WALLY
KATE

500

noul,

P. 211 lying
P. 206 few
P. 280 yield
P. 282 discomfort
p. 144 Gandhi
p. 203

P. 87

Compulsive Overeater

Compulsive Overeater

by Bill B.

The basic text for compulsive overeaters

CompCare® Publishers

Minneapolis, Minnesota
A division of Comprehensive Care Corporation

(Ask for our catalog, 800/328-3330, toll free outside Minnesota
or 612/559-4800, Minnesota residents)

Excerpts quoted from *Alcoholics Anonymous,* © 1939, and *Twelve Steps
and Twelve Traditions,* © 1952, 1953, by Alcoholics Anonymous World
Services, Inc. Reprinted by permission of Alcoholics Anonymous World
Services, Inc.

Library of Congress Cataloging in Publication Data
B., Bill, 1931-
    Compulsive Overeater

    Bibliography: p
    1. Obesity — Psychological aspects. I. Title.
RC552.025B2   616.3'9806   80-70095
ISBN 0-89638-046-7   AACR1

Inquiries, orders and catalog requests should be addressed to
CompCare Publishers
2415 Annapolis Lane
Minneapolis, Minnesota 55441
Call toll free 800/328-3330
(Minnesota residents 559-4800)

11   12   13

88   89   90

Acknowledgments

When I entered Overeaters Anonymous (OA) in 1970, I never thought I would encounter the love and inspiration I found, not only to lose weight and keep it off, but to write this book. I found others, too, who took a genuine interest in my desire to gather together these writings in book form. I appreciate *so much* what they and Overeaters Anonymous have given to me. I cannot name them all, but they know who they are.

However, I want to give special thanks and love to my sponsor, Doris S., who was always there for me when I despaired, and to Pat Z., Jean S., Judy K., Bernice L., Mitch K., Carole J., Don L., Sandy B., Myra K., Lou A., Patricia H., Daphne D., Ann G., Barbara L., Carol G., Carol W., Robb H., Beverly R., and Rozanne S., the founder of Overeaters Anonymous, and to all those thousands of OAers who came, listened, and shared with me their experiences, strengths, and hope.

I am especially grateful to the fellowship of Alcoholics Anonymous, whose years of help to us in OA gave us the courage to go on, and to the creators of the Big Book, who opened my eyes to the wonders of their freedom.

Also, I could not have even started this book without the support, understanding, talent, and love of my wife. She stood by me during the insanity, cried with me during the recovery, and shares with me any credit of accomplishment.

Contents

The Twelve Steps

Adapted for compulsive overeaters

Step One
We admitted we were powerless over our food compulsion — that our lives had become unmanageable.

Step Two
Came to believe that a Power greater than ourselves could restore us to sanity.

Step Three
Made a decision to turn our will and our lives over to the care of God, as we understood Him.

Step Four
Made a searching and fearless moral inventory of ourselves.

Step Five
Admitted to God, to ourselves and to another human being the exact nature of our wrongs.

Step Six
Were entirely ready to have God remove all these defects of character.

Step Seven
Humbly asked Him to remove our shortcomings.

Step Eight
Made a list of all persons we had harmed, and became willing to make amends to them all.

Step Nine
Made direct amends to such people wherever possible, except when to do so would injure them or others.

Step Ten
Continued to take personal inventory and when we were wrong, promptly admitted it.

Step Eleven
Sought through prayer and meditation to improve our conscious contact with God, as we understood Him, praying only for knowledge of His will for us and the power to carry that out.

Step Twelve
Having had a spiritual awakening as the result of these steps, we tried to carry this message to other overeaters, and to practice these principles in all our affairs.

The Twelve Steps reprinted for adaptation by permission of Alcoholics Anonymous World Services, Inc. Copyright© 1939.

Editor's Preface:
Please Read This First

Since *Compulsive Overeater* is based upon lectures and workshops given by Bill B. at different times and in various places, readers will notice an informal tone and some repetition of themes and anecdotes. Compulsive overeaters can find help by reading the chapters either in sequence or separately.

Compulsive Overeater is one person's interpretation of the Twelve Steps of Alcoholics Anonymous (AA) especially as they apply to the problem of compulsive overeating.

The Twelve Steps, first developed by AA, have become the basis for many other Programs which deal with unmanageable problems and compulsions — Al-Anon, Alateen, Overeaters Anonymous, Narcotics Anonymous, Emotions Anonymous, Emotional Health Anonymous, Gamblers Anonymous, Parents Anonymous, Families Anonymous and others.

This book is not intended to replace the Big Book (titled *Alcoholics Anonymous* and published by Alcoholics Anonymous World Service, Inc.) as a resource for Twelve Step Programs. Bill B.'s interpretation of the Twelve Steps comes from his own dedicated reading of the Big Book and from applying the Twelve Step principles to his own life.

This interpretation of the Twelve Steps may not be

everyone's. Bill B. can only share how the Program has worked for him — first to help him find happiness and serenity, and second, as a by-product, to help him lose seventy-five pounds and maintain his weight loss for over ten years. If this sharing helps others find what he has found through the Twelve Step Program, it will give him joy.

Those familiar with the steps will deepen their understanding through this book. Those unacquainted with the Twelve Step principles may want to explore them further by becoming part of a Twelve Step fellowship or by reading the Big Book and other Twelve Step literature.

Compulsive Overeater was written and published independently of Overeaters Anonymous and therefore has neither the endorsement nor opposition of OA.

Excerpts from *Alcoholics Anonymous* (the Big Book) and *Twelve Steps and Twelve Traditions* are reprinted by permission of Alcoholics Anonymous World Services, Inc. The page references to the Big Book are from the Third Edition, seventh printing, 1980. The page references to *Twelve Steps and Twelve Traditions* are from the nineteenth printing, 1980.

Author's Introduction

It seems that all my life thin people have told me how to lose weight. All I needed was willpower, they said. "You're so nice looking, but you should lose weight," or "You have such a pretty face" are familiar phrases to overweight people, meant to inspire us to use the willpower to lose weight. Unfortunately those "inspirations" never gave me the power to do anything.

In the long run, the only thing that ever stopped me from eating myself into oblivion was the honest sharing from other compulsive overeaters. Only they really understood my dilemma: I needed the power to lose weight, but had little, if any, power to resist that first compulsive bite.

I always believed that if I could be thin I would be happy, that I was unhappy because I was fat, and that if I exercised some willpower, I would lose weight and be happy. But what I didn't know was that I was not a happy person *inside* — fat or thin. People who are happy do not abuse their bodies by compulsively overeating.

We compulsive eaters don't feel bad because we're fat; we use fat as an excuse for not feeling good about ourselves in the first place. We have been programmed to feel bad and all our willpower is expended to serve that purpose. We need some apparently logical explanation for our programmed bad feelings.

Food and fat are convenient and instant excuses.

Many of us compulsive overeaters sabotage our own efforts to lose weight and keep it off. Losing weight forces us to consider reality because we no longer have the old, reliable excuse for being miserable. We find we cannot handle happiness. The pressure is unbearable and we therefore prefer the relative safety and comfort of being fat and unhappy.

We have a fundamental problem which is larger than the inability to handle food wisely. Our problem is that *we believe* that we can do what all those thin people advise us to do — exercise willpower — when we have a *total inability* to exercise that power when it comes to food. We are powerless, so we choose short-term coping programs. These may be suitable for normal people, but not for us. These programs feed our self-pity, create feelings of deprivation, and so send us scurrying back for a binge. We feel like we have failed again. I got tired of that frantic dieting-bingeing cycle and finally decided that it was not what I wanted. I wanted to live life, not just cope for a time and feel empty and deprived.

For me, the answer came from an unexpected source: a fellowship of people, a powerful book, and a program of spiritual growth that changed my life forever. These things have become so important in my life that I often forget that not everyone is familiar with them. A brief introduction:

Overeaters Anonymous (OA) — A self-help group adapted from the original concept of Alcoholics Anonymous, a fellowship of men and women who come together and share how they work a program of *recovery* to solve the common problems of overweight and unhappiness in their lives. OA was founded in 1960 by several people who saw the principles of the Twelve Step Program working in the lives of others besides alcoholics. Starting with one small group, OA has grown in twenty years to more than five thousand groups in twenty-two countries throughout the world.

Alcoholics Anonymous — A book written in 1939, known affectionately as the "Big Book." This book was written by recovered alcoholics and is still recognized as the basic text for the group, Alcoholics Anonymous (AA), and other groups, including Overeaters Anonymous, which use adaptations of the original AA Twelve Step Program. The recovered alcoholics who wrote the Big Book did so in order to show precisely *how* they had recovered. I take my direction from this inspirational group of people. The purpose of my book is to share with other compulsive overeaters exactly how I have recovered.

Twelve Steps and Twelve Traditions — Another Alcoholics Anonymous classic. This book, in explaining the Twelve Step Program, characterizes the steps as "a group of principles, spiritual in their nature, which, if practiced as a way of life, can expel the obsession . . . and enable the sufferer to become happily and usefully whole" (p. 15). The Twelve Step Program is one of single purpose that deals with an illness which is threefold — physical, emotional, and spiritual. The Program, however, is first, last, and always a spiritual program. These steps are still as inspired, as effective, as uncompromising and practical now as when they were first put in writing over forty-five years ago.

Working the Program means following the Twelve Steps in everything you do. There are two other terms which have special meaning for compulsive overeaters: *inventory* and *abstinence*.

Inventory, referred to in the Fourth Step of Alcoholics Anonymous as a "searching and fearless moral inventory," is a thorough self-analysis, a listing of the aspects of one's character.

Abstinence for the alcoholic, of course, means refraining from drinking any alcohol (or using any mood-altering chemical). Since overeaters cannot forego eating entirely, abstinence for them is open to different interpretations. For some overeaters, abstinence means eating three balanced meals a day and giving up refined sugar and flour. Others develop their own abstinence — cutting out the kinds of foods that seem to be weight-producing for them. For me, however, abstinence means freedom from food compulsion, that is, being free of the desire to eat compulsively.

There is no substitute for the Big Book. For me, nothing could ever replace that book as a guide for recovery. Yet when I was a newcomer to OA, I found it difficult to relate to this book. Since I was not an alcoholic, I thought the text was difficult to understand and not really relevant to *my* problems, though it was interesting. Only after years of pain, spiritual need, and coaxing did I come to understand the Big Book and hear it speaking directly to me.

By sharing my experiences with the Big Book, I hope I might somehow shorten, for others, the time necessary to see and really *feel* the promise of the Program. *Compulsive Overeater* is not meant to replace the Big Book in any way. Each of us must use the Big Book text in our own way and find in it what we need. Instead, my book is an account of my recovery from compulsive overeating through the use of the Big Book and the Twelve Step Program. I have organized the material which follows to correspond with each of the Twelve Steps and with some specific, universal subjects. Throughout, it remains an account of my own experiences, interpretations, and conclusions.

When I began recounting my experiences for this book, I thought back to my first OA meeting in 1970. It was there that I first heard the term *compulsive overeater.* I resisted that label; I disliked being told what I was by a group of strangers. The suggestions I heard at the first meeting seemed more like demands and I rejected them for that reason. It took me a long time to realize that the help offered to me then was the benefit of other people's experience.

I was first motivated to lose weight because I thought being thin would finally make me happy. I was offended by the group's suggestion that I had to change my thinking; that a weight loss, by itself, wouldn't solve my problems or bring me happiness. I came to OA wanting only to lose weight. Communicating with a Higher Power and reaching out to others held no fascination for me at all. I just wanted to achieve a weight loss for myself — once and for all — and then run. But something began to happen to me in that group and my life will never be the same again.

As far as I am concerned, reading the Big Book is the most important thing that has ever happened to me. At first I felt a little objective curiosity about the book, but I really didn't understand those people who wrote it. I had never been an alcoholic, I didn't relate to their drinking problems, and I certainly wasn't ready to accept a "Higher Power" as the route to my happiness and weight loss.

The time came, however, when everything else in my life failed and I became willing to find a new path, a new way to obtain meaning for my life. Over and over again I was directed by others on the Program to seek the answers in the Big Book, so I read and re-read the stories in the book. As I read, the words seemed to reach out to me. I had come to believe that happiness was forever unobtainable — or if it was obtainable, I had seen no proof. But I saw through their stories that those alcoholics had what I wanted. I didn't relate to their drinking, but I surely related to their sobriety. They had lived lives similar to mine, though their symptoms were different. They showed me that happiness was obtainable.

All I had to do was do what they did. They promised me abstinence from compulsive overeating forever if I became willing to live the Program each day in all my affairs. *Spiritually* was not a useless term, but a word given to explain the otherwise unexplainable and miraculous recovery they had experienced and for which I yearned. If I practiced those twelve principles, they said, the God of my choosing would allow me to have an incredible change in my state of mind. The person I had been would no longer exist; in his place would be a recovered, sane, happy man. I followed those directions, working the Program and practicing the Twelve Steps, and as a result, the quality of my life is better than I ever dreamed possible.

The foreword to *Twelve Steps and Twelve Traditions* says, in effect, that the principles of the AA Program can work for anyone. I believe that the purpose of the AA Program is to regain sanity through practicing a Twelve Step approach to achieving a change in one's state of mind. That is a "miracle" and can only come from an unexplainable source, which I choose to call God.

It is important to remember that the Big Book was written by many recovered alcoholics. For them *recovered* means that the compulsion to drink was taken away. This is not to say that these people never again thought about drinking — some did and some didn't. I *still* think about eating compulsively at times. The difference is that now I don't have that uncontrolled urge to act out my thoughts about food.

Happiness is a by-product, a gift that comes to us *indirectly* through our thoughts and actions. But our insanity gets in the way by telling us to *pursue* happiness, and we usually respond with some kind of indulgence. If you find that you've overcome one compulsion only to switch to another, you're not living the Program. We must learn to substitute positive action for all compulsive behaviors. The Twelve Step Program tells us exactly how to do that. The answer is here in the steps, if we're just willing to accept them and allow them to work in our lives.

The Twelve Steps guarantee me sanity if I commit myself to them. We were created to be happy; when we choose to be unhappy we're really going against nature. The symptom of our dysfunciton is that fat we see on the outside. We are distorting the body God gave us because we are distorting the life He gave us. The sole purpose of the Twelve Step Program, as I know it, is to bring about spiritual contact with God as I understand Him. When that happens, not only will I lose weight, but my *desire* for food will be removed.

This Twelve Step Program cannot be worked selectively. You either work it in total — all the steps — or you don't work it at all. There's nothing magic about the number of steps, except for the fact that together they work! The Twelve Steps give me the real option of saying "no." That's the difference between yesterday and today for me. I now have the conscious choice I lost years ago. I choose God's power instead of my own and I get the power of choice in return. The key to eternal happiness can be found right here in this Twelve Step Program. But if you insist on doing things your own way, this Program will not work. Remember, your way got you here in the first place. This is not a diet program; this is a save-your-life program.

Bill W., the co-founder of AA, brought the Twelve Step Program to life with his realization that he had to carry the message to another alcoholic in order to save himself. Believe me, the same holds true for dealing with other compulsions. In order to save ourselves, we must carry the message to other compulsive overeaters. We can't just sit around and wait for the phone to ring. We save ourselves by reaching out to help others.

The foreword to the second edition of the Big Book says that strenuous work of one compulsive overeater with another is vital to recovery. I'm grateful that I read and understood that passage, for it set me straight about the purpose of the Program. When I first heard this was a suggested Program, I assumed that meant I didn't have to do much of anything. Of course there's a difference between reaching out to help people and doing things *for* them. I believe in helping people to help themselves. We carry the message, not the person.

Go out there and learn to overcome any fear or frustration you might have about talking with people. If you don't reach out, you're wasting time with this Program. Nobody's perfect. We need to risk sharing our simple message with others and the way we do that is to tell them about our lives. This is a program of attraction. An individual's exposure — direct or indirect — to a sane program of recovery means that his or her life will never be the same again.

I like being thin better than being fat. But being thin is another by-product of this Program, not the major result. At one meeting, I was pleading with people to be *willing,* just willing to give the Program a chance and have faith that it would work for them. Their response was, "Yes, but we're fat and we want to get thin first!" This brought to mind a poem from *Through the Looking Glass* by Lewis Carroll, who in his writing made symbolic references to his own drug addiction.

I'll bet you remember the beginning of this . . . but perhaps not the end:

> *"The time has come," the Walrus said,*
>   *"To talk of many things:*
> *Of shoes — and ships — and sealing-wax —*
>   *Of cabbages — and kings —*
> *And why the sea is boiling hot —*
>   *And whether pigs have wings."*
>
> *"But wait a bit," the Oysters cried,*
>   *"Before we have our chat;*
> *For some of us are out of breath,*
>   *And all of us are fat!"*

What the Walrus is saying, I believe, is that the time has come for us to talk about life and living. And the Oysters' response is, "Just a second . . . after all, we have this infirmity — we're compulsive overeaters. We're not ready for life, because we're fat!"

That's the usual cry of compulsive overeaters, who are inclined to put off *living* until that day — sometime in the future — when they lose their extra weight. The truth, however, is that we can begin to live the very day that we become *willing* to give up compulsive overeating and to work the Twelve Steps.

Compulsive Overeater

My Story

After more than thirty years of compulsive overeating, I finally put together a theory about myself that still rings true: somewhere between not eating at all and eating everything I want is the appropriate behavior for me. Applying that theory to my own life, it took me another three years to discover that only God can remove my compulsions.

Food became very important to me early in my life. As a child, I quickly learned to associate eating with feeling good. The systems of reward and punishment that developed in my young life just reinforced that eating-feeling good association. "Be a good boy and finish your supper!" As a very young child, I was required to sit at the table until I had finished everything on my plate — no matter how long that took. I soon concluded that eating was a good thing for me to do; that, futhermore, if I did what I was told — namely, eat — people would like me! So I developed a special taste for certain foods, along with a shortcut to feeling good. I found it wasn't necessary to rely on other people in order to feel good; I could reward myself with those favored foods and have good feelings instantly! I'd say to myself, "You're entitled to have a cookie" or "Go on, take that piece of candy." My mother kept the *real* goodies locked up. I stole the key and perfected a thrilling triple-play: steal the goodies, reward myself, and put one over on mother. Lying and cheating in order to feel good seemed appropriate at the time. Moreover, as I grew, I set out on a path of doing whatever was necessary to feel good, regardless of the outcome.

This feeling good — whether for a minute or a day — was worth most anything to me. It provided short-term relief from a very real and persistent sense that I was a bad person. Of course, I almost always got caught in the act of my lies and my cheating. In fact, I often figured out subtle ways to *insure* that I'd get caught. You see, after the rush of feeling good had passed, getting caught and feeling bad connected with my negative sense of self. Thus began an interplay of behavior and consequence that would make my life miserable for years.

Other than occasional flashes of feeling good about food and deception, I was not in touch with life through feelings. As a child, I built elaborate defenses to protect myself from the beatings my mother inflicted on me and from rejection by other children. Feelings of love, joy, sorrow, and anger were all but unknown to me. In fact, it was only recently that I cried for the very first time in my life.

Children have a strange way of getting even with their parents. I would never give my mother the satisfaction of crying when she hit me; I'd just sit there and take it. I also became the stooge, the scapegoat for other kids. At times, I'd sit in a chair for hours, resisting attempts of others to make me move or talk.

When I chose to be active rather than passive, I always reacted inappropriately. Someone would hit me and I'd laugh; then later I'd pick up a brick and hit someone else — usually an innocent bystander. My teachers thought I was retarded and I, too, believed something was terribly wrong. Finally, I was sent to a school for problem children. I accepted being sent away and the sense that I was being punished — both the fact and the feeling again confirmed my "badness."

I was a clumsy, chubby kid. At thirteen, I was six-foot-one and weighed over two hundred pounds. That also happened to be the year I was sent to live with relatives in California. I attended a regular public high school in Los Angeles, got by, and began to have glimmers of insight about the way I had cut myself off from the world. After a while, my parents and two sisters moved to California and we lived together as a family again. It seemed to me that my sisters got all the benefits. As a boy, I was less perfect, less important.

Though still convinced that I was a bad person, my new-found success in school had changed dramatically one part of my thinking. If I could get one A in school, then I could get others. Knowing that I actually had the ability to change my performance was a very exciting prospect. I had been stuck at one extreme, meeting others' expectations of me by acting dull and unresponsive. Now, determined to explore the other extreme, I made plans to attend college and establish a straight-A record there. And I did it! At the beginning of each semester, I'd talk with each one of my teachers about requirements for an A grade. Then I'd systematically set about to meet those requirements, and more. I was compulsive about it; anything less than a perfect grade was just not acceptable to me.

During college, I began to take an interest in my appearance and first experimented with dieting. I'd put on fifty pounds and take it off each year — like some sort of annual ritual. I'd just pick out the latest fad diet, follow it to the letter and it always worked for me. I never found a diet that didn't work . . . you eat less, you're going to lose weight. Just makes sense. Of course, what I called dieting is the way thin people eat normally.

Time to get married, I thought. After all, I was eager to leave home and marriage was obviously my ticket out. Even with my degrees and supposed intelligence, I couldn't quite see that if leaving home was what I wanted, all I had to do was move. I was sure marriage would give me the happiness I was seeking. But there was lost time to make up for in establishing relationships. I'd never had a date or serious discussion with a woman, much less a relationship with one.

As it turned out, I married the first woman I ever really dated. We met at a dance and I figured it must be true love when she asked me to call her sometime. Why else would she want to see me again? She must love me, I reasoned, and who was I not to love her back — this beautiful girl with the kind of nice, loving family I'd always wanted for my own. Besides, weddings were terrific — talk about feeling good! The weddings I'd been to were great celebrations. I felt sure that was exactly what I needed to be happy, to feel complete — a wonderful wedding followed by a great marriage.

Law school was the next goal I set for myself. Not only would a law degree confirm the fact that I was smart, but the money I'd make as a practicing lawyer would surely reaffirm my worth to the world. It didn't take long, however, to discover that my degrees and my law practice were not going to make me happy.

About six months after the wedding, the joy and novelty had long passed and I realized that I wasn't really all that happy with marriage. The next message came to me loud and clear: if your wife can't make you happy, then having a family will. So we had a couple of children. Now I truly had it all: degrees and a high-status profession, wife, kids, a beautiful home, and a big car. All the indications of intelligence and wealth in place and on display for the world to see. But amid all these symbols of success, I was really miserable.

Strange as it sounds, new shirts gave me more pleasure than anything else at that time. Buying shirts was my sophisticated new shortcut to feeling good. Each new shirt would give me a moment of happiness, a great good feeling of starting over. I had a closet full of them — there must have been a hundred shirts — all reminders of a restless, unhappy time in my life. That was, in fact, the precise time that could serve as an example to people who might think that happiness comes with having everything desired . . . or with losing weight. I had an abundance of material things, but these proved to be merely the symbols, not the reality, of happiness.

I finally decided that if the conditions of my life were not going to give me happiness, then I'd have to find it another way. So, on to a series of affairs with other women and a period of really reckless spending for clothes, cars, and a new house. And, as always, I got caught. But I didn't care; getting caught confirmed, once again, that I was compulsive and that I was bad. It was almost a relief to get in touch again with those feelings of worthlessness. Divorce seemed to me like the logical next step, but my wife made the first decisive move — she kicked me out of the house with only the clothes I had on and my car. She felt that was all I deserved. And that was relief too, being rejected and divorced by my wife. That's exactly what I felt I was entitled to; I didn't deserve to have good things happen in my life. I was now legally free to pursue the irresponsible life I'd been living for the past three years. And now I lived it up as never before. I acted out my fantasies and ignored my children. I got a beautiful apartment, had exciting people around me all the time, and access to drugs and the immediate highs they produce.

After three more years of this carelessness, something happened that could only be described as a gift from God. Suddenly, I had an overwhelming desire to straighten out my life. I remarried. I walked away from my fantasy living, started seeing my children again, and took some responsibility for their needs. It appeared that I had completely reversed the direction of my life. I kicked my drug habit, started making money again, accumulated possessions, began to gain back the respect of my colleagues. In many ways, I was getting a second chance. But I never got another chance at all with my mother or my older sister. At the time of my marital break-up, both sisters had sided with my ex-wife against me. Not understanding how they could reject their own flesh and blood, my mother refused to speak to her daughters again. She soon died of what I'm convinced was a broken heart. My past behavior had destroyed a relationship between others and, quite possibly, had shortened my mother's life. Again, confirmation that I was bad, unworthy, probably unfit to live. More and more, I thought about suicide as a reasonable way out.

For the second time in my life, I had it all — yet was so miserable I felt ready to choose death. Then my obsession shifted and focused in, once again, on my weight. At six-foot-one and two hundred and thirty pounds, I was not exactly obese. To me, however, the excess I had felt like five thousand pounds. My weight was choking me. Now I was convinced that my overall appearance — specifically my weight — had been keeping happiness from me for all these years. I had tried all the weight reduction methods — diets, shots, pills. I always lost the weight . . . and gained it right back again. I kept saying to myself, "One more diet, one more inspiration and I'll be geared up, really ready to do it . . . " My life, to this point, had been a series of half-hearted attempts to find happiness. All I had really learned was how to be more sophisticated in my insanity. I was traveling in the wrong direction down a one-way street, trying desperately to twist the street signs so they'd meet my expectations.

But God *does* work in strange ways. Just at the point of my deepest despair about weight, I happened to see a former secretary of mine. She'd been overweight when I worked with her, but looked terrific now — lean and healthy. I asked how she made the transformation and she said, "OA." That was a new one to me. She told me where the meetings were and even offered to meet me there. Now, this was a very clever lady. For while she told me the address of the meeting place, she said not one word about the building itself. When the address put me in front of a church, I thought there must be some mistake. No, the lady had played a dirty trick on me. She knew that churches and God and religious concerns were just not my style.

For some reason, though, I went in and took a seat in the back of the room. Was *I* in the wrong place — the only man in a room of fifteen women! This was going to be very uncomfortable for me and I was going to quietly slip out of the room as soon as possible. Then, one woman in the group caught my eye. She had a glow of happiness and a serenity about her that intrigued me. She seemed to glide across the room as she took her place before the group and began sharing her life story. I simply could not believe what I heard her say. This gracious and attractive woman had been a prostitute, an alcoholic, a drug addict, a compulsive eater. Still fascinated, I spoke with her briefly after the meeting. She sensed my interest in the Program and directed me to some literature on a table in the room. I took the literature. I was going to work this Program, at least give it a try.

I lost weight very quickly and found that attending meetings helped me — most weeks, I'd show up three or four times. Finally, one night I stood up and spoke at a meeting, mostly because it was a great way to get positive strokes from people. I started speaking a lot at meetings. There I'd be, telling the group how I'd been in the Program for three weeks and lost so much weight. And the people would actually be listening to me and applauding. They didn't have a clue about the kind of person I *really* was. I can honestly say that was the first time in my life I believed anybody actually wanted what I had. These people who were listening and applauding were not interested in feeding my ego; they wanted me to give them hope. If I could do it, maybe they could do it, too. This kind of reciprocal relationship with other people gave me the first inkling of what the Program was really all about. I continued attending meetings and continued losing weight. After three months of participation in OA, I had lost seventy-five pounds. I'd never been thin in my life; my lowest adult weight had been 182 pounds. Now I was there, I was thin — 165 pounds — and feeling a little uneasy about the unknown.

Before I knew much about sponsors in the Program, I assumed that they'd be kind of surrogate parents, telling people what to do and when to do it. But they're not like that at all. My sponsor, in fact, helped me to stop blaming my parents and others and to take responsibility for my own life. He'd been on the Program for some time, had this wonderful serenity and absolutely no intention of controlling my life in any way. He claimed I had choices and that whatever I did was completely my responsibility. My sponsor never tried to pull me along in the Program, never prodded me to write my inventory or share at meetings. Instead, he told me how those things had helped *him* grow in the Program. The decisions about myself and my own growth were clearly up to me. But with my sponsor's help, I came to see myself more clearly as time passed.

When I first wrote my inventory, I had a real problem with the concept of God. I came to the Program with a certainty that there was no Higher Power, no God. All that existed for me was a rather absurd life and a knowledge that I would die one day. As I began to grow in the Program, however, I found it necessary to at least develop willingness to believe in a Higher Power. That willingness is absolutely fundamental to the Program. I didn't actually have to believe but I had to be willing, open to the *possibility* of a developing belief.

As I worked the Program, all kinds of first-time experiences began opening up to me: sharing with others, showing affection and, finally, a sense of believing. I began to find serenity with God and even led a few retreats. But I still had a lot of personal pain at that point, still was not being totally honest with myself. And the OA people were on to me. Initially, they'd be attracted to my story and what I was saying, but I couldn't keep them interested. As a sponsor, I couldn't even sustain a helping relationship beyond a week or two. I was sure that my Program was somehow defective.

Food continued to have a powerful hold on me long after I got thin. Not wanting to risk gaining weight again, I developed a concept of food as the enemy. This gave me an opportunity to use my energies for a fight. And that fight made me rigid in my attitudes. I laid a batch of rules and unrealistic goals on the people I tried to sponsor. But that simply didn't work. Rules and goals don't free people from food — they merely transform an obsession with eating to an obsession with not eating. Unhappiness creeps right back in there to fill up the void — the time formerly used for eating.

Finally, my own sponsor suggested that we look to the Big Book for help. He was sure an answer could be found there, and it was. For while I had understood the Twelve Steps and had shared them enthusiastically with others, I hadn't honestly accepted the steps myself. My ego, my pride, and a basic insanity were effectively blocking that acceptance. First of all, for an intelligent, successful man to say he's powerless over a simple food compulsion seemed ridiculous to me. Even more absurd, I thought, was the idea that a God out there somewhere was actually going to take care of me. Furthermore, how could I confess my wrongs? I'd be more than happy to help other people confess theirs, though. The inventories I wrote weren't mine at all, but a composite of other people's inventories, attempts to say what I thought was expected of me. Asking God to remove my character defects seemed like wasted effort. I truly didn't see that I had any *real* defects. Oh, I'd had the weight problem once, but that was taken care of. Perhaps now I didn't have enough popularity or money, but those were minor defects compared to the ones I heard about in others. I'd had experiences with making amends so that step, too, seemed rather ridiculous. People in the Program would get up and tell about something they'd done when they were eight years old and recently made amends for. And it was so good, they'd say, because after making amends, they'd go home and find an unexpected refund or something in the mailbox that would help to pay the rent they were worried about. Not me . . . under similar circumstances, I'd come home to an eviction notice. Or, I'd make amends to someone and they'd say, "It's about time," without any sign of appreciation.

But, in spite of all the doubts and reluctance I felt, I gritted my teeth and tried to work the steps. There was no alternative for me now. I wasn't quite sure what was happening, but one thing was clear: I could not go back. I simply could not return to what I had been. It became a physical thing. I actually felt physically ill when I tried to go back and do things the way I used to. My sponsor would ask me about my inventory. I'd question why I had to write one and he'd simply say, "I don't know, but that's what the book says and it should work for you." I'd say, "Well, I'm not going to write mine." Then the anxiety would build up, along with some physical pain and I'd choose to write my inventory. Something was pushing, pushing me on and telling me there was no alternative. Now I know that a special energy moving me forward was my sanity — God working his will in my life.

Sometimes we do things because we're told there's a reward at the end. Often, though, just doing those things becomes a reward in itself. I found some great rewards along the way as I began to change my behavior and started making amends to people right away. I was driving one day when, because of a blind spot in my sideview mirror, I cut somebody off. Well, that driver honked and honked and gave me dirty looks as he pulled up alongside me. As God works things, though, there was a red light and I had to stop. The man started cursing me. I opened my window and said, "You're absolutely right, sir. I didn't see you and I apologize."

He just looked at me and said, "Oh! Well, in that case, I apologize for honking at you." That's the way it happened! The goodwill between us was almost automatic. Furthermore, funny as it sounds, my admission of wrong and my apology meant I didn't have to worry about dinner that day.

I maintained my seventy-five-pound weight loss for three and a half years. But I was going to leave the Program at that point because I was still obsessed with food each day of my life. It was a constant struggle not to eat compulsively. Then I read the story about Dr. Bob, the co-founder of AA. It took two and a half years before the obsession for alcohol was removed from him, even though he did not drink during that time. Dr. Bob's story renewed my faith and trust that the obsession for food would eventually be removed from my own life. I forced myself beyond reading the Twelve Steps and into action. No matter how tired or lazy or unprepared I was, I wrote my inventory. I worked hard at believing.

When AA was first organized, Bill W. wanted to make the Twelve Steps mandatory. He was talked out of doing that, though, and compromised by establishing the steps as suggestions. Later he said that it was the best decision he ever made; mandatory steps would have driven away millions of alcoholics needing help. He came to realize that compulsive people try to get even when they're *made* to do something. And, getting even backfires — often taking those people back to old behaviors and obsessions. People in AA believe that there is only one way they can truly stop drinking and that is to have the obsession with alcohol taken away. Similarly, I believe there is only one way I can stop eating compulsively and that is to have my obsession with food taken away. Literally, I must lose my appetite. If I don't have an appetite for chocolate cake, I'm not going to eat it. Intellectually, I know what I can eat and what I can't. I know that eating too much will make me fat. The problem is, that even having these facts doesn't help a compulsive eater stop. Only a loss of appetite does that. And only God can take that appetite away. Back to that chocolate cake. I just don't eat chocolate cake anymore and it isn't because I'm afraid. If I wanted it I'd eat it, but I feel no desire. In fact, I have about as much desire for chocolate cake today as I have for rat poison. It just doesn't interest me. God has removed that obsession.

I'm not claiming perfect abstinence for myself or anyone else. I don't think perfect abstinence from compulsive overeating is humanly possible, at least for any substantial period of time. That would mean not eating more than you should, not eating forbidden foods, not eating too fast, not feeling you have the need to eat at certain times of the day. My abstinence is imperfect; I still have a lot to overcome. There are still times that I eat too much, still times I put on three to five pounds, almost overnight. Now and then I fall back into my old behavior of eating too fast and getting hungry by the clock. Before I came to the Program, when I was really compulsive about food, I'd come home after work to an evening of snacking. All day, I'd fantasize about it — passing time with goodies and television. What else was there? I've since found many interesting, productive ways of filling my evenings without filling my stomach.

I have had a food compulsion and it comes back to me all the time. It is only removed by God when I work the Program. When I was eating compulsively all the time, I just couldn't bear to throw out even the tiniest bit of food. Have you ever tried throwing out a piece of cake? It can feel like losing an arm . . . it's like death. Occasionally, I still fight that feeling.

Working the Program applies to all aspects of my life, so it's really more accurate for me to speak of *living* the Program. I have a simple but reliable way of knowing when I'm not living the Program in all areas of my life: the appetite returns. Sometimes, I'm not even aware of it at first. I'll start eating more, eating faster and on a strict schedule. Then, I'll step on a scale and see I've gained a pound or two and that's clear warning to me. Or maybe, on finishing a meal, I'll realize that I didn't even taste the food. That's another sign of compulsive eating that I watch for.

As I grow in the Program, I see God as the most important thing in my life — without exception. Abstinence or freedom from compulsion is God's gift to me and I get it in exact proportion to the degree that I live the Program. Each day, I get better and better. Each day, I feel more in conscious contact with God. Each day, I have spiritual experiences that simply cannot be described adequately. Those experiences aren't terribly dramatic; they're more like warm feelings that cover me and fill me with strength. This Program is a living program and its primary goal is to allow participants to live spiritually fit lives. I came to the Program having controlled my compulsive eating. The Program took me much, much further and helped me stop *wanting* to eat compulsively. And that, God knows, was the tougher battle and the greater victory.

Step One

"We admitted we were powerless over our food compulsion — that our lives had become unmanageable."

I want to share with you my experiences with Step One. The First Step was very hard for me, as I'm sure it is for everyone. I was not going to admit that I was powerless over anything. Maybe other people's lives were unmanageable, but — except for quirks and other people's faults that got in my way — I was very good at managing my life. If the world would only listen to me, I thought, my life would work out and so would everybody else's.

I really believed I was very adept at managing things. The problem was that somehow I didn't always get what I wanted. But I thought I just needed a little bit of luck here and there. For instance, when I was dieting I always knew I could have finished losing the necessary weight — except that certain events prevented me from reaching my goal. A holiday would turn up just when I had five pounds left to lose. That was unfortunate and unlucky.

The First Step of the Program tells us that we are powerless over our food compulsion and that our lives have become unmanageable. It doesn't say we are powerless over being fat or over eating compulsively. Alcoholics don't say that they are powerless over being drunk. They say they are powerless over that substance out there called alcohol. We are totally powerless over what food does to our bodies. When it comes to food, we act insanely. We have no power. It's very simple. But when I first came to this Program, I had never really accepted this. That's what taking the First Step is all about.

All along, I thought I wanted to be thin, and all I had to do was follow what thin people did. Could I live the way I had been living and still be thin? No, it doesn't work that way.

I looked at the way I ate and saw that it wasn't the way thin people ate. Thin, sane people do not eat when they are not hungry. Thin, sane people aren't hungry right after they've eaten. Thin, sane people don't come home from work and have a sandwich before dinner. They don't eat two or three cakes at one time. But I did all those things.

I abused my body and I abused food. The insanity was not so much that I abused food, but that I thought I was normal. After years of suffering, I finally began to hear what all those people in the Program had been saying when they talked about Step One: I was insane when it came to food.

The beginning of the Big Book contains Bill W.'s story. Bill W. talks about reaching a certain point at which he realized that nothing in his life worked. Nothing he did seemed to give him what he wanted — peace of mind and happiness.

I want to talk for a minute about two different feelings. One is feeling "good" and the other is feeling "happy." Feeling good for me was just short of not feeling bad. A day that was not too painful was a good day to me, so I called that feeling happy. "Well, I got food today and no great tragedy occurred," I would think. That was a happy day for me. I never believed I could feel real happiness. At the moment that I was eating I felt good, but after eating I always felt the pain, the guilt.

Someone once told me that he had stopped drinking alcohol and had found that not drinking was less painful than drinking. In the same way, working a program of abstinence is less painful than the results of eating compulsively. The good feeling that comes from overeating isn't worth the bad feeling that comes afterward. We feel guilty, angry, and depressed when we eat compulsively. We are masochists. We put ourselves down because we overeat, saying, "There, I did it again and as long as I did, I might as well just continue to eat."

At some point each of us confronts a tremendous hurdle. We face the ordeal of *not* eating compulsively, the pain of pushing something away and saying, "I'm not going to eat that." This is very difficult for us and we are able to do it only when the pain of eating is greater than the pain of not eating compulsively. This comes at a different time and place for each one of us.

The pain of compulsive eating became so great for me that I was willing to do anything to get rid of it. That's what must take place. It's called "hitting bottom." Nothing in the world can convince a person to work this Program until he or she hits bottom. People say to me, "Bill, I'm willing to go to any length — I can't stand it any more."

I ask, "To any length?"

They say, "Yes, of course."

Then I ask, "Does that mean you are willing to do whatever I suggest to you?" When they say that they are willing, I know they are ready to hear about the Program.

The Big Book was written by people who decided one day that even if it meant walking in front of a speeding auto, that's what they would do to get rid of their pain. They'd do it because nothing could be worse than the horror of where they were.

When I came into the Program, I hurt badly enough to begin working the steps. I knew that my weight had gotten me where I was. My way of doing things was the reason I was there. Nobody dragged me in, nobody pushed or forced me. The way I worked my life had gotten me where I was — but I wasn't willing to admit that yet. I was always looking for easier, softer ways to do things. I figured there had to be one more way hidden somewhere in the recesses of my mind, something that would allow me to control the world. I always figured wrong.

I thought maybe those people in the Program were right and maybe they weren't. Maybe Bill W.'s way would work and maybe it wouldn't. But at least I had a chance. Anybody else's way was perhaps a chance for me. My way had no chance — I had worked all my chances out.

I thought I had come into the Program to lose weight. I believed that I ate too much and became fat and that because I was fat, I felt bad. If I lost weight, I would feel good, I thought. So I dieted. I lost weight. But I still didn't feel good about myself. The truth of the matter, it later became apparent to me, was that I had always felt bad — I had been programmed to feel that way and to look for excuses. Whether I lost weight or not, I would still feel bad about myself. What I had to do was work on feeling good about myself.

It seemed strange that in order to feel good about myself I had to admit my powerlessness over myself and admit that my life was unmanageable. My life didn't seem unmanageable to me — after all, I had accomplished so much. However, from all my accomplishments I had been unable to obtain the one thing I wanted most: happiness.

We are willing to admit that we are fat, obviously fat, and we say that's because we can't control our eating. So, logically, what we think we need is to be able to control our eating. And what better way to control eating, we think, than to have somebody work with us in controlling it? The relationship with that person will be so embarrassing and we will want so much to belong to the group that we will exercise the discipline that we need to diet.

But the Big Book tells us that we are unable to accept our devastating weakness and all its consequences. One of its consequences is that we are not like normal people, nor will we ever be. We have the *inability* to control our eating.

Dieting is controlling our eating. But I cannot diet honestly because I am a compulsive overeater. I cheat. I am a liar because I cannot deal with food — I would rather lie than eat honestly. I can't stop, which is why I fit the definition of a compulsive person. I can't stop myself from taking either the first bite or the last bite. I can't even stop in between. I have an inability to control my eating.

Some people put on weight and can diet whenever they need to. It's no big problem for them, as they are normal people. Normal people can do that. But we cannot do that because it is universally true for us that we are powerless over our food compulsion.

There are many people who lose weight and then put it right back on. That is not the goal of this Program. The goal is to learn how to accept ourselves and feel good about ourselves. The Program tells us that God will relieve us of the compulsion to overeat. We will lose weight automatically and never put it back on again — but not through dieting.

We come to the Program thinking that it will teach us how to lose weight, but the Program has nothing at all to do with that. In fact, people can have the disease of compulsive overeating whether they are fat or thin. Our disease is not just a physical phenomenon. Being bodily fat is just one symptom of a disease which is emotional and spiritual in origin. We are not in the Program to lose weight; we are in it to stop eating compulsively. There is a big difference.

The First Step talks about giving up the battle of trying to control things "out there." When I stop trying to control everything — wishing, hoping, forcing, cajoling, threatening — I become free to deal with myself. Because of that, I learned, a day would come when I would feel good about myself. When I feel good about myself, when I am happy, it is impossible to overeat. Now I really believe that God didn't make me out of junk and that I no longer have to hurt myself or abuse myself by putting junk into my body. I don't have to be an unhappy person anymore.

Some of you may say that's okay for others, but it won't work for you. You point to troubled lives and families and jobs. Let me tell you, your problems come from inside you. You are what you are, whether you accept it or not. You will get whatever payoff you want. Fat has been one of our payoffs — but it doesn't have to be anymore. This Program is a chance for you. Anybody who has trouble losing weight, anybody who is gaining weight after being thin can find relief in this Program. You will automatically be thin.

We have to get rid of the part of us that says we're no good, we're wrong. Once we begin to accept ourselves just as we are — with our mistakes and imperfections — our lives begin to change. We can search for love, but in the long run the only important love is the love we give ourselves. When we love ourselves, we can function and live the way we were created to. How can we love others when we are all wrapped up in our own unworthiness? We have to stop reflecting other people's moods and opinions and just be ourselves. We cannot control others or let them control us.

What makes this Program difficult is that it is the exact opposite of everything we have been taught. We have been taught to be strong, to have discipline and willpower. Now in the First Step of the Program we learn we are to give all that up. We hear that in the process of giving up our control, we will get what we want.

Most of our lives we have been trying to control things. We try to control tomorrow and — what's even more ridiculous — we try to control yesterday. How can we learn anything new when our minds are so filled with yesterday and tomorrow? How can we be ourselves when we are trying to be everybody else? We're so busy worrying about how things should be, what everyone around us should do and say, that we are unable to live in the here and now. If we say we are powerless over everything out there, admit that our lives have become unmanageable, it's like really being free for the first time.

In dealing with problems, I sometimes have to take the First Step literally a hundred times in a day. The only problems I have in life are those which choose to have, those that I manufacture for myself in order to feel bad. When I realize that I have no power to change people, places, or things out there, the problems are relieved.

I used to think that if it was cloudy or raining out it was going to be a trouble-filled day for me. I found out that the weather has nothing to do with whether a day is good or bad for me. I used to let other people or things control my life. I found out it doesn't have to be that way anymore. What other people do is their problem. I am powerless over my family, my children, my employer, the weather, the traffic, money, relationships. I want to live each day to its fullest, because all I really have is today.

I used to be afraid of living. It was very difficult to live in the present because I was one of the "walking dead" — always living in the past. Many people are like that. We are like wind-up toys — our past winds us up every day. When people say that I remind them of someone, I say I don't care about it. I am me. I'm not the person they think I remind them of. Living in the past isn't going to work today.

The chapter on Step One in the book *Twelve Steps and Twelve Traditions* calls alcohol (or, in our case, food compulsion) a tyrant and says that it wields a double-edged sword for us. It says that we were first "smitten by an insane urge that condemned us to go on drinking (overeating), and then by an allergy of the body that insured we would ultimately destroy ourselves in the process."

That was very significant for me. When I read it the first time, I realized that I had this insane urge (though I had kept my weight off for a long time) and that I would never change.

Normal people can eat chocolate cake and chocolate malts and sandwiches. Their bodies are not affected by those foods. But I have abused my body for many years, so I cannot eat cake or candy or sandwiches and still keep my weight down. It may be due to allergy or disposition or heredity — I don't know why, and it doesn't really matter. The point is, that's the way I am. Nothing is ever going to change the effect food has on my body.

Food affects my brain, my thinking process — and then I get fat. I don't like being fat because it is uncomfortable and unhealthy. Since I know I cannot change the effect food has on my body and since I don't like being fat, I know I cannot eat certain foods. That's the way it is, and it has become a fact that I accept.

It may not seem fair that we cannot eat the way we used to. But that's like saying that it's not fair that I have black hair. When I was a child, I always wanted to look like the kids down the block who had pug noses, freckles, blue eyes, and blonde hair. I was the fat kid with brown eyes and black hair. For so many years of my life I felt I would do almost anything to be like those other kids — but all the wishing in the world wasn't going to give me blonde hair and blue eyes. It was a terrible problem for me then, but it is no longer a problem. I am what I am — and I accept me. Sure, I would like to be able to eat all I want or to be able to order chocolate cake, candy and sandwiches at restaurants, but it can't be that way.

We have to learn the difference between facts and problems. Facts about ourselves become problems when we make believe that they aren't true. Having black hair and brown eyes is a problem to me only if I insist on pretending that I have beautiful blonde hair and blue eyes. But that's what we do when we insist we're like normal people saying, "I can eat all I want. All I have to do is diet and lose weight. Then I can eat pizzas and I'm not going to gain my weight back." I kept telling the whole world I was just like anybody else, I could eat whatever I wanted to. But I was the only one who bought my own lie. Everybody else seemed to know the truth but me.

Now I know that whatever I am is what is appropriate for me. I am a certain age, a certain height, a certain weight, a certain disposition. I choose to be me today — fat or thin.

What the First Step helps us to see is that we are what we are — and we are never going to be different. Before I accepted the First Step, there was always hope in the back of my mind that somewhere, somehow, my body would change and I would be a normal person. I kept telling myself that I could lie a little bit today, I could eat a little more today.

Someone once told me, "Well, I don't eat a lot, but it's okay for me to smoke grass once in a while." Well, it's not okay for *me* to do whatever I want. Working my Program means that I have to conduct all my affairs properly. That means I don't lie, cheat, steal, drive my car the way I used to or do things that are against the law. I have to work my program all the time — not because I'm perfect, but because that's the only way it works for me.

When I first came into the Program, it was just another diet to me. God became my food sponsor as I tried once again to control my eating. But a controlled eating program is just another attempt to have power over my life. If I'm filled with my own power, there's no room for God's power. We have tried diets but the First Step says we are powerless over them. We need to stop overeating *before* we start — because once we start, we are powerless over that insane urge. God took away from me the need to control food by taking away the insane urge.

The Program tells us that we will lose weight automatically, which means that we don't need a program of rigid discipline. I can't be disciplined. I resent discipline. I have to give up trying to be disciplined and let God take care of it for me. Sure enough, it has been taken care of — and that comes from taking the First Step.

I have a library of diet books. They are all very interesting. I used to believe that one of those books was going to give me the word, the inspiration I needed to lose weight. They always did — for a month or so I would go around talking about it and then finally put the weight back on. All those exercises and diets probably do work — but what do you do when you don't want to do them? You could tell me about a terrific diet, but it wouldn't work for me because I have a problem when it comes to dieting: I can't stay on one.

I always knew I shouldn't eat certain foods, but I didn't know how to stop eating them. All the good feelings I got from other people never helped me stop. When I went to work and faced the real world out there, those people weren't with me to hold my hand.

They weren't with me when things piled up and I couldn't handle it all and I wanted to eat. There was nothing inside me to make me not want to eat.

We all think we really want to be normal. We keep saying that we are normal, but actually we are afraid to be like normal people. We are afraid to be just like any other person in the big city, working a nine-to-five job or taking care of the house or getting merely average grades in school. We can't handle that. We have to be noticed. People notice a fat person before they notice an average one. Nobody would notice us if we weren't fat — and that's what we are afraid of. Yet we say we want to lose weight.

In the Program we learn how to be just like everybody else and be unique within ourselves. A feeling of warmth and happiness comes from knowing within yourself that you are unique. You know there is only one person like you — but you don't have to prove it to anybody. All along we have been trying to prove we are special by saying, "Hey, notice me, notice me. Look how bad I am. Look how big I am."

I don't have to be noticed all the time anymore. In fact, my practice now is to yield the right-of-way in everything. If people want to get in front of me on the freeway, they can go ahead. How can I get angry at them if I let them in? When I'm in a market and someone is in a rush and wants to get in front of me, I step back. People can go ahead of me anytime. I will yield the right-of-way. If you and I argue and you want to win, you've got it. I can't get angry if I *let* you win. I don't want to argue anymore. My favorite mottos now are "So what?" and "I yield the right-of-way." That's the state of mind we have to achieve.

I thought I was a winner in life because I had money and prestige, but I was a loser. I lost everything I touched. I was a loser because I felt like a loser. You are what you feel. I felt I was a loser in everything and it showed. My friends were losers, my family were losers, the kind of work I did was a losing job.

I spent so much time and energy proving that I was the best or the worst at everything I did. Now I don't have to be the best or worst anymore and it's a load taken off. I really feel good about myself and my work. The people I work with tell me that I've changed. My work is more reliable because I am more reliable. It didn't happen until I could see myself as I really was, until I came into the Program and was willing to offer myself without reservation.

Watch children: they run around and have a good time when they love themselves. They are happy and they're not fat. Happy kids don't get fat. Happy kids don't lie. Happy kids don't steal and cheat. Happy kids don't hit other kids. They play and they enjoy life. They don't feel bad about themselves. We eat compulsively in order to continue feeling bad — that's our payoff. If we don't want the payoff, we won't eat compulsively.

The Program tells us our situation is fatal. We must realize that the disease is killing us, just like alcoholism kills the alcoholic. Until we accept that, the Program will not work for us. My problem was my obsession, which happened to focus on food. Because of my state of mind, I would have taken up something else if I hadn't taken up compulsive overeating. I couldn't stop eating — or hurting people or hurting myself or being depressed or angry. People told me how terrible I was and I still couldn't stop. I understand now when somebody says, "I can't stop."

The first thing we have to do as we approach the Program is to admit our pain and realize that we are powerless over our food compulsion. We must see that our lives are unmanageable. The willingness to accept the First Step every day of our lives from now on is not a burden. It releases us from the bondage of ourselves.

Step Two

"Came to believe that a Power greater than ourselves could restore us to sanity."

This step caused a big change in my life. "What is this restoration of sanity all about?" I wondered. The Program first tells us to give up our problem, and then it says that if we give up the problem, God will restore our sanity.

This is not an easy idea to grasp or to believe in. Some people in this Program claim I talk nonsense. "Don't listen to Bill," they say. "He talks about being relieved of his compulsion — in other words, being sane. We can't be sane," they insist, "because we're crazy people!"

Well, what does Step Two talk about? It says God will restore us to sanity — if we're willing. God *will* restore our sanity. If you've never believed anything else, believe that. The Big Book promises you — just as it promised me — that God will take away your compulsion. You do not have to have it anymore.

When someone asks, "Have you eaten compulsively in years?" I answer, "NO!" That person says, "Well, I still feel as though I want some ice cream." That's normal! Most people feel as though they want ice cream or miss one food or another. So what?

We glory in being sick. We say, "I'm a compulsive overeater! I have found a label for myself that explains all my craziness before." We love to be sick — until that day when we look at ourselves and say, "Hey, I can't take it anymore. I refuse to."

I reached that point in my life — I refused to take it anymore. People had told me about the Program. I didn't like everything I heard, but there was no other place for me to go. Now I know that it doesn't matter whether I liked what I heard, because I have learned that the Program is right. If you want to be crazy and use this Program as a diet, I hope that will work for you. I don't want to work the Program at that level. I want something else. I want more out of life than to spend the rest of it being crazy. I cannot believe that if there is a God in heaven he wants me to be unhappy or to be a practicing compulsive eater.

After years on this Program, I know it's still the same world out there. I still get ripped off, I still lose things, and I still have problems. But somehow I just glide through it now. I feel better than ever about my life. Of course, I still have down days and up days. I get depressed and I harbor resentments. I get angry sometimes, but it doesn't last long and seldom do I act on it.

Now I call my sponsor to say, "Hey, I had a terrific day today. I dented my car and lost my wallet, but I still came through it." It used to be that if things didn't go my way, it was time to get angry. That was just a good excuse. I knew how to justify everything I did, how to blame everybody and everything for my feelings. I never ate a thing that somebody else hadn't made me eat. I kept saying, "If you hadn't done that, I wouldn't have to eat! If you hadn't done that, I wouldn't be angry! I wouldn't be depressed if it weren't for you!" Now I know that we can't afford to have that kind of self-righteous anger. We can't afford to have resentments. And we don't have to have them.

Most of us compulsive overeaters have been in the gutter emotionally all our lives. We come to this Program and we lose a hundred pounds. Then we're not in the gutter anymore, we're on the sidewalk. From the sidewalk, the gutter looks like it's a million miles away, although it's only really a step away. If I come along and say, "Hey, how about coming up to the penthouse with me?" some people say, "Don't jeopardize me here on the sidewalk. I mean, don't jeopardize my Program, Bill. You know, you're talking crazy. You scare me. I don't want to take a chance, because if I get up on my own two feet I might fall back into the gutter."

That's exactly the risk you have to take. I was willing to take that risk, and there are others who are willing to take that risk. They don't just want to make it from the gutter to the sidewalk and stay crazy, they want to go to the penthouse! I tell you, we're entitled to it! I'm entitled to be up there! That's where I want to go and I'm going to work at it to the best of my ability each day, one day at a time. I'm a compulsive overeater, I have this terrible disease, but I want to walk upright like a man. I choose to go to meetings and work the

Program because I find it is of assistance to me. Your compulsion is going to end if you work this Program.

There are people who work the Program and never binge again. They never put weight back on again. They have totally relieved themselves of food. The refrigerator is not buzzing in their ears all the time. They don't worry about what they should eat or how much. From Day One on this Program I don't deal with food. But if someone wants to go get a diet, I tell that person to go ahead. It doesn't make any difference because if we work this Program, it all happens automatically anyway.

Newcomers ask, "What is the reason for doing it this way?" And I tell them, "God will restore your sanity." That's why. However, you can't have your sanity restored unless you accept the fact that you are not sane. You might as well leave if you think you have sanity already. You don't need to stick around because the purpose of the Program is to *restore* your sanity.

To me, sanity is being able to live my life and enjoy it without having to worry about food or people or situations, without worrying about things or the desire for things or letting things out there control me. Sanity means eating in a normal way — not through discipline but through accepting myself as I am. Sanity means having relationships with people *even though* I'm afraid. Sanity means being willing to risk. Sanity means living my own life, not somebody else's life, and it means living in the present rather than in the past. Sanity means being the cause of my life rather than the effect of other people's lives. Sanity was what I wanted all along, but I never knew it.

People seem to talk more about diets at meetings than about sanity. Sometimes the talk all seems to be about *insanity*, in fact.

Some say, "Thank God for my insanity. Thank God I'm a compulsive overeater because otherwise I wouldn't have been led to this Program." Maybe that is true, but if I could have had this Program without having gone through the tortures of bingeing, guilt, compulsion, and everything else that goes with being a compulsive overeater . . . well, that would have been nice.

Once when I spoke at a meeting, an older fellow who was at an OA meeting for the first time in his life asked me, "How long have you been on the Program?" At that time it had been five years. He said, "And you still come to meetings?" I said, "Yes." He asked, "How often?" I replied, "Well I go a couple of times a week." Then he asked "Why do you need that kind of a crutch?" And I said, "Well, it's kind of like the way I got here. I live in California and I came to New York to speak. I flew here. I could have walked, but it was a lot easier to fly."

I don't have to go to meetings. I don't have to call my sponsor. I don't have to read the Big Book anymore — but all of those things sure make my life a lot easier. If you can't see, it's a lot easier to get by with glasses. We love to do things the hard way, don't we? It doesn't have to be that hard. God *can* restore our sanity.

God saw fit to give me what I call a Pinocchio Syndrome. You remember Pinocchio — *every time* he told a lie, his nose grew. Well, every time I *lived* a lie, my *body* grew. Every time I stop working this Program, I wake up in the morning *feeling fat*. It has nothing to do with what I *ate;* it has to do with what's in my head and the step I refused to work the day before. When I'm not working the Program I get to feeling fat and get to feeling bad — and the vicious cycle begins again.

The Second Step gives us the first promise of the Program, an immediate promise: that God can and will restore us to sanity — if we choose. That's important. What sense is there in working this Program if there is no promise? God restores our sanity by removing the desire to eat compulsively. Our appetite is gone. The drunk who says his appetite for alcohol was removed didn't do anything. God removed his appetite, restored his sanity. That's the kind of sanity I want. I have come to believe that a Power greater than myself can and will restore my sanity — and in fact *has* restored it. It does happen, and it should happen to you. If you still have an appetite or compulsion, you're not getting what this Program promises. If you don't get that, you're being shortchanged.

The Second Step is a step of faith. We have to come to believe. I say *have to* because if we don't believe, we just won't get what the Program promises. The Program does not demand that we do anything. The Twelve Steps are suggestions, not requirements

— but it takes faith to make them work, to believe that God will restore us to sanity.

You may find it hard to swallow Step Two all at once. That's okay. Looking back, I find that I took the steps piecemeal myself. All you really need in this Program is a desire to stop eating compulsively and an open mind. You don't need to debate the steps — just try them and see how they work for you.

In *Twelve Steps and Twelve Traditions* we read, "Step Two is the rallying point for us all. Whether agnostic, atheist, or former believer, we can stand together on this Step. True humility and an open mind can lead us to faith and every meeting is an assurance that God will restore sanity if we rightly relate ourselves to Him" (p. 33). That's the promise of the Program . . . that God will take away our appetite if we rightly relate ourselves to God now.

If you could dig deep down inside your soul and be honest with yourself, I know that some of you would say, "I hear what he says, but I really don't believe that there is some Higher Power out there that will automatically take away my appetite. I don't believe it." Until you are *willing to believe,* this Program will be just a social diet club for you. You have to hurt enough to say, "I don't know whether it's true or not, but I'm *willing* for it to be true." You've got to *want* to believe. Then you have taken the Second Step.

I went to meetings for years and heard how the Program works. Yet I didn't *really* hear for a long time. Now I never get tired of hearing it. I believe God speaks to us through people. I listened to people talk about Step Two at meetings, but I never really heard the words "came to believe that a Power greater than ourselves could restore us to sanity." I think the reason I couldn't hear was that for a long time I refused to believe that I was insane when it came to food. In order to be restored to sanity, I had to acknowledge that I was insane.

When I acknowledged my insanity, then I really became depressed. I said to myself, "My God, I'm insane when it comes to food. My life is unmanageable." That's where the Second Step comes in. Right away I was given the promise that if I acknowledged my *insanity*, there is a power greater than myself who will restore me to *sanity*.

We intellectualize, we try to figure everything out. "Why is he saying that? Who is he to say that?" All I know is that the Program works for me and for a couple of million drunks and compulsive overeaters. Are you so unique that it won't work for you? Instead of trying to figure out why it won't work, just try it! We must keep our minds open, and that only comes from hurting. When we hurt enough, we take the First Step, and then we can get into the Second Step. We must see that we have an insanity of the body, mind, and spirit first. These steps are in perfect order. First they knock our feet out from under us and then they hand our footing back to us. And that's just the beginning.

I never took any class called Happiness 1A. I was taught history and geography, but nobody taught me how to be happy. I literally didn't know how to be happy. I didn't know what to do when I was thin, either. I'd never been thin and nobody gave me a class in thinness.

How do you dress thin and look thin and carry yourself thin? I didn't know. Have you ever seen fat people sit in chairs? They don't sit, they slump. Thin people sit differently. They sit erect and they have a certain style that others can see.

Do you know how thin people eat? What we call dieting is the way they eat. Did you ever talk to a thin person who was eating? Thin people put down their forks and talk to you. I wouldn't have sat and talked while I was eating in the first place. I couldn't do two things at the same time — and eating took precedence over all other activities. If I had to meet somebody for a dinner appointment, I ate first because otherwise I couldn't concentrate on what happened at dinner. No one knew I had already eaten. When I ate, I had to eat every bite. I couldn't let any food go to waste. After all, I was paying for it. God forbid it should go to waste.

Sometimes people I sponsor come to visit me in my office. I'm in the corner of the twenty-sixth floor and my windows overlook an area common to several office buildings. I ask people who come in to go over to the window and look down. I tell them to notice the winners and losers down there just by the way they walk. How we feel about ourselves permeates our lives. We're not just losers because we are fat — we are losers in everything, and it shows. The crazy thing is that we don't have to be losers. But we buy that because we don't know how to be any different. I didn't know there was another way. Intellectually I knew there were thin people who were happy, but inside I wouldn't believe that there was a Power greater than myself who would restore *my* sanity.

A very great philosopher summed up his theory of life by saying, "I look at the universe around me, I see what works, and then I do it." I sat up in the middle of the night once, thinking, "Why don't I do that?" I know what makes a relationship happy. Why don't I just look at people who have happy relationships and do what they do? If I want to be thin, I've got to look at a thin person and see how that person lives — really lives and then live that way.

Sometime people say, "I don't want to change. I'll lose my spontaneity and my gregariousness." We're always afraid that if we change, we're going to lose something. I found out that the only thing I lost was my weight and my insanity. I never lost anything worth keeping. As a matter of fact, most of me that I lost I should have lost a long time before.

We think there are things we "have to do" in order to have God come into our lives. Many people — and I was one — talk a lot about God, about a Higher Power, but they're only giving lip service. The more I talked, the less it worked for me. Quality of faith is more important than quantity. The more I was just willing to believe and allow the Program to work, the more it happened.

The Program is really a threefold process. First, you understand that you are insane when it comes to food and many other things; second, you have faith that

God will restore you to sanity; and third, you learn through ten other steps how to relate to God.

I've learned that the Program is a spiritual one. The Program works for me only through the grace of God. I know lots of people get other things in other ways from the Program. I did it for years. I worked the Program through "my willpower." But this is a spiritual program and I don't think there's really anything else to talk about. As a matter of fact, someplace in the Big Book it says "That's what this book is about — it's about a Higher Power."

What I've learned through this Program is that I can't do certain things by myself. My human power has failed. Only God can do for me what I haven't been able or willing to do for myself. I have come to believe what the Second Step promises: that a Higher Power really can restore my sanity.

Step Three

"Made a decision to turn our will and our lives over to the care of God, as we understood Him."

It was very difficult for me to form a concept of God. I kept thinking God had a big beard and sat up there pointing his finger at me and saying, "You rotten kid, you." That's how I understood God.

When I came into the Program, I tried several different concepts. But first, I had to be willing to investigate — to say, "Okay, I don't believe there is a God. If there is one, fine. Show me. I'm willing to see it." I had a lot of doubt, but I was willing. I had an open mind about it. Since then God has revealed himself to me in strange ways. My concept has changed.

I found a practical way to form a concept of God, a way which was easy for me and which also seems to work for other people. First I imagined what kind of God I would want *if* there were a God, and then I became *willing* to have the kind of God I imagined and to let that God take care of things for me.

A woman I sponsor came to see me one Friday. She told me, "Everything's working terrifically except this God concept. I've got a concept of this horrible punishing God, and it's not working."

I said, "You can choose your own God. If you want a God, what kind of God would you like? Just think about it a minute." As she thought, she started smiling. I asked, "Why are you smiling?"

She said, "I would like to have a God like the good witch in *The Wizard of Oz*. The one with the sparkles and the wand."

That was fine with me. Who can say what God looks like? We all have images. Maybe God is a woman or a little boy. For that woman, God was a nice witch with sparkles and a wand. I said to her, "Okay, close your eyes and think a minute. What would your God say to you?" She said her God would say, "You're okay. You ate too much yesterday, but don't worry, it will work for you. You're a beautiful person."

I said, "That's a good concept! Why don't you just think about that over the weekend and see how it works? Every time you have a problem and want to talk to God, take that image and just stick it up there."

She called me Monday to say she had had the most incredible weekend. Every time she had a problem, she made believe the God she had imagined was there, and it worked. I don't *know* if there is a God. Nobody *knows* if there is a God, except by believing. Believe and He exists. Try it. It works.

My concept of God is a little different from that woman's. On one of my shoulders sits a little God who looks like me with a halo. That God says, "Bill, don't worry. Everything is going to be okay. If you do something wrong, I'll love you anyhow." When I have a problem, I talk to that God, who says, "Well, Bill, you have a couple of choices. One of those choices will make you feel good temporarily, but in the long run the price you pay is going to be heavy. The other choice is uncomfortable in the beginning because you don't like to do good things for yourself, but it will feel better in the long run. Why do you want to feel bad?" When I decide to feel bad, this God is never going to say, "See, I told you so." Instead he says, "Okay, so next time we don't have to do it that way, right?"

On my other shoulder there's another look-alike of me — except for the long tail, pointy ears, and pitchfork — who says, "Go ahead, you can have a bite of that. Go ahead, you can go seventy on the freeway — don't worry about it. You'll get away with it this time. After all, you're in a hurry, and how many times have you gone that fast and not gotten caught?" Sometimes I listen. More often, I don't. I believe God sent the little devil on purpose. This way I will never forget where I came from, where I can be anytime.

I believe there is no universal figure of God. Nobody knows what God looks like. Your concept of God is just as good as the next person's, so why don't you make up your God? I guarantee it works. God is really a belief, a faith.

I see God in other people's faces all the time. When I say the Lord's Prayer at the end of a meeting, I don't close my eyes and look down. I look in other people's faces, because that's where I see God.

God is different to each person. If you want God to be a woman, a man, a child, a little thing on your shoulder, or a fairy princess — hey, why not? If you have faith in your concept of God, it works. To me, that's what the Third Step is all about: I made a decision to turn my will and power over to the care of God *as I understood Him.*

I've worked on this Third Step for so many years that I thought I knew exactly what it was all about. Then one day I read this passage on page 36 in *Twelve Steps and Twelve Traditions:* "If I keep on turning my life and my will over to the care of Something or Somebody else, what will become of *me?*"

We think we are going to become a nothing, like the hole in the doughnut. But, if we read further, we see that this kind of thinking ignores an important truth: "Dependence, as [the Program] practices it, is really a means of gaining true independence of the spirit."

Those words were the key to freedom, but I never understood them. I was brought up with the idea that you didn't become dependent on anything or anybody. I didn't need any help. Well, I *do* need help — from people, from this Program, from God. I can't do it by myself.

I need contact lenses because I need help to see. I need the help of an airplane to get somewhere. It's cold, so I need the help of a jacket, I need the help of heat. I need lots of help — so why can't I acknowledge that I need help with my spirituality?

The Big Book says, "We have not only been mentally and physically ill, we have been spiritually sick . . . When the *spiritual malady* is overcome, we straighten out mentally and physically" (p. 64).

I kept thinking that if I lost weight I would be happy with myself, and then I could be very spiritual. I couldn't be spiritual and fat, I thought. It's like saying, "When I get rich I'll learn to do this; I can't afford to do it now." I always did things backwards. I thought that if I lost weight I would feel good. I didn't know that if I felt good, I'd lose weight. People who are happy do not get fat. They do not abuse their bodies.

According to page 45 of the Big Book, "Lack of power . . . was our dilemma. We had to find a power by which we could live, and it had to be a Power greater than ourselves . . . That's exactly what this book is about." That's exactly what this Program is about. I can't fit two powers in one place. When I have my power, there's no room for God's power. When I let go of my power, God's power fills me up. The person I used to be was full of wind — hot air.

The purpose of this book, these steps, this Program is to enable you to find a "Power greater than yourself which will solve your problem." In the Third Step, giving the problem over to a Higher Power relieves the problem. Just say that there is a God and He exists. I am relieved of the burden of the problem, and I have so much time that now I can go out and enjoy myself.

You see, we do the footwork in carrying out our Program. But how can we do the footwork if we're wrapped up in a problem? The Big Book promises that

God will restore us to sanity, which to me means that God will remove the compulsion and take away the ordeal of trying to solve any problem.

Emotionally I was like a broken record with a scratch on it. I kept going over the same thing: "I've got to eat, gotta eat, gotta eat, can't tell the truth, can't tell the truth, don't trust people, don't trust people." All those messages that I had picked up somewhere else stayed with me. I was stuck and I couldn't move. But a power greater than myself picked up the tone arm and moved it on. Why? Because I gave up trying to justify and rationalize and let God take over.

The more dependent I become on a Higher Power, the more independent I am, the more freedom I have. God restores me to sanity. Yes, it's that simple. I hurt so badly that I was willing to believe, then I believed, then I was free.

I have to take that Third Step over and over again, many times a day, whenever I am uncomfortable, whenever I have a problem. It always works. I have blind, unadulterated trust in a Higher Power. Sometimes it's just little things that happen, like getting parking places when I'm not supposed to. But incredible things — even miracles — happen when we have faith.

Decide what kind of God you want. For a long time you've made your spouse or your parents or your children "God"; you've made food your God. Having a God shouldn't be any problem for you. Why don't you make "God" something worthwhile? Just try it out. Make up your own personal God. Then you *can* turn your will and life over to the care of that God. God can be something so fantastically wonderful. I tell you, it *works*.

There's a story about a man who climbs a mountain. He's just about to reach the top when all of a sudden there's nothing to grab onto. As he reaches out, he slips and starts to fall. He looks down and sees a five-thousand-foot sheer drop. Just as he's about to fall, he grabs onto a branch. He's holding onto the branch for dear life, but the branch starts to give way. This man doesn't believe in God, but he figures now is a good time to begin. He says, "Is there anybody up there?" He just hears the wind blowing and the branches crumbling and getting looser and looser. He says, "Please, is there anybody up there?"

All of a sudden he hears this voice saying, "Yes, my son, I'm here."

He says, "My god, is that God?"

The voice says, "Yes, this is God, my son. I will take care of you. What is it that you want?"

The man says, "I'm going to fall. Please help me."

God says, "All right, my son, let go of the branch."

The guy looks down and says, "What did you say?"

God says, "Let go of the branch."

The man asks, "Is there anybody else up there?"

You see, that's exactly what we're asked to do. We're asked to let go of everything. That's why we're told this is not going to work unless we're really hurting. Only a person who is really hurting is going to let go of the branch. The rest of us are going to try to scheme and figure out a way to stay where we are —

and we usually do. We get by. It's only when we're really hurting that we take the drastic step and decide to have absolute faith.

Step Three says, "Made a decision to turn our will and our lives over to the care of God as we understood Him." But our understanding of God is often part of the problem. Now, who wants to turn our will and lives over to some punishing God, some angry God, our parents' God? I don't want that kind of God.

Even atheists have the "punishing God" image in their minds. I say to them, "Look, what kind of a God would you like there to be?" If they answer, "But there isn't one," I suggest they forget that "there isn't one," forget about their old concepts, and just make up a story about a terrific God. I tell people to make believe for a moment that God exists. What kind of a God would that be? Make one up and see what happens. After all, we make believe lots of things. The form of your Higher Power is just not important.

We don't really know for certain what the future holds in store for us. We have had experiences in the past, and based upon those experiences, we think we know what's going to happen to us. But we don't know — nobody does. It's the same thing with God. We've lived so many years with an image or non-image of God. Maybe every time I had faith in God, I got kicked. I'd go home and find the check I'd expected wasn't in the mailbox, or I'd receive terrible news. So I thought it would always be like that.

When I believed there was no God, I got nothing. When I believed in a loving God who had nothing else to do but follow Bill around and take away his appetite, that's exactly what I got.

I wanted a God of trust and I wanted to lose my appetite. I wanted many things. I listed all the things I wanted, even those that were ridiculous. Then I became willing for that God to be there. The kind of God I imagined created within me the ability to be sane. God had the power to give me the things I had always wanted in life, the things that were going to make me happy. I didn't know that God would go about it by making me happy *first*, and that all those other things would come automatically.

The most incredible miracle happened as soon as I made a decision to create a loving God. By believing a God could exist, I had the opportunity to have all the things I fantasized having, be all the things I wanted to be. It worked. I am the kind of man I always wanted to be. Within each of us is a God-given ability to imagine our own personal God.

Sometimes the image of a punishing God comes back. But every time I get that image I say, "I don't want to believe in you. I want to believe in a good God." I force myself to think of a beautiful God. I look in people's faces and I believe.

It was a tremendous relief to look in the mirror and know that my God looked just like me, was with me in anger, was with me in fear, was always there, was always in everybody else. It was also a relief to know that God didn't judge me as good or bad.

God sometimes says, "You know, I told you there was another way, but you insisted upon doing it your way. Why do you want to do that when there is another way?" But he also says, "It's all right, it's okay, I like you. I'm not going to punish you."

So I began to have a little trust. Then came the second part of Step Three. It was to "turn our will and our lives over to the care of God." And that was hard. Our problem: we are compulsive eaters but think we can eat like normal people. That problem is what we can turn over to God. The *how* to turn it over is exactly what we are told in the Big Book. We must be *willing* to give it up, *not to live in the problem.*

Life becomes a problem when we continue to think that it's going to change and we act as if it should change. If you have a spouse who is an alcoholic, or children who don't appreciate you, or parents who treat you as if you're four years old, or a job for which you're being underpaid, you've got to accept that as fact. Your wife or husband is not going to change. Your kids are not going to change. Your parents are not going to change. In fact, the world is going to be just as awful out there whether you are thin or fat.

Let me tell you, *nothing* is going to change and we have to accept that. The traffic won't separate for us to pass. No miracle. When I fly, I don't get a first class seat. No one says, "Oh, here comes Bill. Put him on the plane first class, right by the captain." When I drive home, I get the same traffic that everybody else gets coming home from the airport. I know that I cannot change my wife, my children, my parents, the world. I am free at last from the need to try to change them.

I am free. I know that I don't have to manipulate food. The five-hundred calorie piece of cake is no longer three hundred calories. It is five hundred calories and that's no problem. I can't make magic anymore. What a load that was to carry. I don't have to worry about what I eat anymore. I know it's all no good for me. So why bother with it? I just wipe it out. It's fattening to me.

I am willing to allow God to direct what I eat, how I drive, how I talk to people, how I deal and react. I am willing to allow God to be in control. Now I don't have to figure out what there's going to be for dinner and how much I should eat and whether everybody is going to watch what I have on my plate.

I can begin to think about such mundane things as enjoying life. I never knew how to do that. First of all, I never had the time, because my mind was always busy worrying about how I was going to control this and control that. I would manipulate, weigh, measure — but it never came out right because invariably the world is the world is the world. What a relief to give up trying to change it and begin living my life. I have become independent of the problems because I accept the facts as they are, including what I am: I am a compulsive overeater, I'm 6'1" and have brown eyes — that's the way it is.

That's the significance of the Third Step. It's the willingness to give up the battle. It doesn't say you *have* to give up anything. You can keep all the problems you want. You can try to manipulate. Nobody says you have to give that up. Step Three just asks us to be willing to allow this image of God to direct our lives.

The greatest miracle for me is me. To know the kind of person I was and to see each day the kind of person I have become is the greatest miracle to me since the creation of earth. I see the living proof — and it happened because I was willing.

A passage from *Twelve Steps and Twelve Traditions* deals with this idea of being willing. It says that once we have acquired willingness, we are the only ones who can make the decision to *exert* ourselves. Trying to do this is an act of one's own will.

The passage goes on to say, "All of the Twelve Steps require sustained and personal exertion to conform to their principles, and so, we trust, to God's will. It is when we try to make our will conform with God's that we begin to use it rightly . . . This was a most wonderful revelation. Our whole trouble had been the misuse of willpower. We had tried to bombard our problems with it instead of attempting to bring it into agreement with God's intention for us" (p. 40).

For me, Step Three has really become what I call the step of trust. There is a big difference between belief and trust. I know that many believe in some sort of Higher Power — they believe in the God of their parents, the God of their religions, the God of their childhood. But having trust is more than just acknowledging God's existence. Having trust is being willing to allow God's existence to overshadow one's own existence.

I trust enough to let go of the branch in the story I related. I know that my God will not let me fall, that I will be safe. I always feel safe and protected, as if I am in God's arms at all times.

Sure, I get scared and I worry, but only when I forget and stop having trust. *The act of letting go is in reality the act of trusting.* We must trust that God will allow us the feelings of well-being and happiness no matter what happens. We may not get the things we want, but we will always get the feelings we want, because what we all really want is serenity, peace of mind, and happiness. Trusting God gives us exactly that, regardless of the external world or how rich we are or how fat we are. Trust and you shall see. Believe in a God who is trustworthy, and that God will never fail you.

Step Four

"Made a searching and fearless moral inventory of ourselves."

The Big Book says that if we straighten out spiritually, the rest of our problems will straighten out automatically. The first thing we need to do is clean house — by taking an inventory of our past behavior. The Big Book suggests that we list things, people, and institutions with whom we were angry and then ask ourselves why we were angry. Go over a chronological history of your life and write down on paper whatever has made you angry in the past. When you are finished you will have a list of your resentments. Read over the list and notice how you have handled people, places, and things in your life. If you are honest with yourself, you will begin to see your own character defects as you recall how you acted in certain situations.

Make a list of these defects. You will find resentment, grandiosity, anger, jealousy, guilt — to name some of them. There really aren't that many character defects. You may list more, but most of them can be labeled resentment or grandiosity.

There's nothing that says you have to do this step. The Big Book says only that these are *suggested* steps.

But I think they are "suggested" in the same way that it is "suggested" that you use a parachute when you jump out of an airplane. You don't have to, of course, but if you don't, that first step is murder.

There are two reasons for doing an inventory. One reason is to uncover character defects. We can do nothing to change until we admit our own faults and ask God to remove them. We will deal with defects of character in Steps Five, Six, and Seven. The second reason for doing an inventory is to look at how we have harmed other people in the past. The Big Book reminds us that this is to be an inventory of *ourselves*, not of anyone else. It doesn't matter what others said or did to us — we're looking only at our own actions here. Steps Eight and Nine in the Program will help us get rid of the guilt we feel for harming others.

I found it hard to write an inventory. I had a lot of trouble with it. I suggest you sit down with paper and a pencil, put the pencil down on the paper, and just be willing to write. Simply close your eyes and scribble. You'll be amazed at what will come. You will see that the words will come if you're willing to let them. When I tried to do an inventory, I did the same thing many people do. I was afraid to start because I was worried about the results. I blocked things out and my mind was an absolute blank.

One thing that helped me get started was doing what I call a prenatal inventory. This is a fantasy which you make up. It will help take away your fears about writing an inventory because you won't have to worry about uncovering painful memories. This is just a fantasy — a fairy tale. Take a piece of paper, draw a line down it, and begin writing on the right side. Pretend that you are in your mother's womb, and then write anything you want to about that experience. Just make it up. Describe what your mother feels about your being born at this time in her life. Write down what your father feels about you, what your brothers and sisters might be saying. Maybe a grandparent lives in the house in which you will be born. Include anything you want to. It might go something like this:

> I was conceived in a moment of great passion during the monthly sexual act between my parents. It was their duty and I was conceived quickly and quietly. I began to grow and slosh around in my mother's womb. My father felt bad about my being born because it was during the depression years. My mother had hoped that I would be a girl because she really wanted a girl. But I was enjoying myself, I was comfortable . . .

It doesn't have to be long — maybe a page and a half or two pages. Just go on through the whole thing. Go through the moment of birth — "Here it is and the cold hands are reaching in to grasp me and they're turning me around and the guy's yanking on my ears and I don't want to be born" or "I want to be born" — whatever comes to your mind, just write it down. Whether it's true or not doesn't matter, because what you write will reveal how you see things right now. Somehow, somewhere, you got those messages. You will see your character defects begin to show up in the story. As you find them, list them on the left side of the page. I've written my prenatal inventory over and over and each time it shows me exactly where I'm at. If I'm feeling resentful, a lot of resentments show up in my story. If I feel inadequate, the story shows inadequacy. Whatever you write down — "they were mad" or "they were scared" — it's really *your* anger or fear that you're talking about. It had to come from inside you because you're the one making up the story.

Go on from there with your story and write about your childhood years — from birth to five years old. Most of this will also be fantasy, because we really don't remember the first few years. At age two or three we begin to have some memories, and by age four we have more. By the time we're five we have pretty good memories. Make up what you don't remember and use memories when you have them. Write a couple of pages. Or if you want to write more, that's terrific. Sometimes people write long dissertations. When you finish, stop and read over what you've written. Again, list your character defects on the left as you see them.

After that, write about the later childhood years, the years from six to thirteen. These are what I call the traumatic years, the period of the most vivid memories. Often you can remember what happened in those years better than you can remember things that happened two weeks ago. A lot of anger and resentment comes from that period. Those years formed the foundation for our compulsive eating and any other compulsions we have. Write down whatever comes to mind as you think about those years. When you finish, look for your character defects in the story.

Continue writing and listing character defects for the teenage years (thirteen to nineteen), the early adult years (twenty to twenty-nine), and the adult years (thirty and older). By the time you get into your teenage years you will probably be bored with your inventory because the same character defects keep showing up.

At the very end of your story, make up something to put on your tombstone. Write your name and decide what the inscription would say. You'll find out that it's pretty much the same thing you've been writing all along. I asked myself, "Quick — what would I say?" I came out with "Here lies Bill, whew, he made it." The way I saw it, life was such an ordeal I couldn't wait to get it over with. That's exactly how my life was.

I guarantee that if you write a prenatal inventory, it will really help. It was the most eye-opening experience I ever had in my life. This kind of inventory really helps remove the fear of writing because there is no fear in writing a fantasy. Lots of us have fears about writing an inventory. We're afraid we're going to divulge something we don't want to look at. You don't have to divulge anything in a fantasy. You don't even have to put down any of your charater defects — they show up anyway. The fantasy just takes away the fear, the uncomfortable feeling that we might reveal a character defect.

One thing writing an inventory shows is that there is really no such thing as writing in the past. We're always writing in the present. Nobody cares if my mother beat me when I was eight years old. What I do care about is why I still harbor resentments about that. If I resent my mother for something that isn't even happening now, can you imagine how I'm handling things that *are* happening now? If I'm a resentful person, my resentment comes out in everything I do. If I feel guilty about what I did when I was six or eight years old, my mind is in a state of guilt and I will feel guilty about things that are happening now or things that I *imagine* to be happening now. The feelings I carry around about whatever happened in the past are feelings that affect me now. They cause my present character defects.

When we carry old feelings around, what we do in the present often has little to do with the "facts" of a situation. For instance, a woman once told me about something that had happened to her in a department store. She was very resentful about it.She told me exactly what happened, but *I* didn't feel resentful about it. The situation itself did not cause resentment. She was upset because somehow she had been programmed to react to that kind of situation. In the same way, I will not be upset if your husband stays out until three in the morning. In fact, it won't upset anybody but you. You might think the most normal, rational thing is to get very upset. But it isn't the *only* way to react. You don't *have* to get angry. The problem we have is learning how to react differently.

How do you change how you react? Well, first of all, you have to recognize what you do in certain kinds of situations. The inventory you write will help you here. My character defects all have to do with how I handle people, places, and things. I know these are defects because over and over again they influence how I act — my actions are based on the wrong motives.

One of my character defects was compulsive over-eating. Another might be anger or resentment — those two really go together. Depression is also a character defect, because depression is really anger turned inward. Depression isn't quite the same as a feeling — it's more a thought process. We feel hopeless and helpless and angry and turn the anger inward. What we have to do is change this thought process.

It's important to see the difference between a thought process and a feeling. You're resentful because somebody took your parking place. I'm not resentful that somebody took your parking place. What does that mean? It means that taking parking places is not necessarily an upsetting thing. It's upsetting to you. The problem is not the parking place or the person who took your parking place. The problem is *you*.

I'll tell you, if there is anything that we are sick with, insane about, it is grandiosity. We can talk about how we had no willpower and we were so meek, but we really were powerful in our weakness. Grandiosity turns up over and over in our inventories. Through your inventory you will realize how powerful you were, how much of an effect you had on your parents and on everybody around you.

The greatest enemies of compulsive overeaters are resentment, jealousy, frustration, and fear. We cannot afford to have these feelings anymore. We know exactly what happens every time we indulge in acting them out, and the price we pay is too high. We must get rid of those feelings. That's why it's important to write down what we fantasize others have said or done to us in the past. Whether they are imagined or real doesn't matter. As long as we believe those things and carry around feelings about them, we will react whenever a situation reminds us of them. Those feelings will have power over us and prevent us from living. I no longer want to be a victim. I want to be the cause of my life.

When somebody I sponsor writes an inventory, we read it through together and then I usually say, "Now go write *your* inventory," because it's often an inventory of everybody else except that person. It becomes an opportunity to dump — "I don't want it . . . you got it . . . you keep it if you want to . . . I don't want it." You know, the way to get rid of all that from the past is to get rid of the reasons we want to hang onto it. We seem to love keeping those little stories of how terrible our lives were. So what if your life was terrible, or my life was terrible? We're not there anymore. We're here now. Let's get all that out so we can see how ridiculous it really is.

Step Four in this Program is where the action begins. The First, Second, and Third Steps are really steps of faith. Step One deals with honesty with oneself — we see ourselves as we really are. Step Two immediately gives us hope. And Step Three is the step of trust. We become willing to let go of the branch and fall. In Step Four we begin to take action.

Lots of people say they have mental blocks about writing. I know all the reasons you can give yourself if you don't like to write — there isn't enough time, I don't know what to say, and so on. But what I hear is that you are afraid of what you're going to find out. Our minds have ways of censoring things to prevent us from dealing with real problems. I was afraid of the results of writing my inventory. I was afraid that I might find out that I could accomplish things. I was afraid I might find out that I could fail. I was afraid of everything. When I learned to like myself, then the fear disappeared. We don't have to write the perfect inventory or make a big production out of it. I think the important thing is to do it.

While fear may be part of the problem, I think most of us don't write inventories because we're lazy, we're procrastinators. That's part of our disease. We put off until tomorrow what we're unwilling to do today, in the hope that it will disappear.

The reason we write inventories is so that we can see where we are now. Sometimes it really hurts a lot to see our character defects and to recognize the messages we got early in life and still carry around with us. It makes us want to cry. But writing an inventory can be a breakthrough — the beginning of a whole new life.

Step Five

"Admitted to God, to ourselves, and to another human being the exact nature of our wrongs."

Step Five is an opportunity to deal with our wrongs. We talk about "giving them away" by admitting "to God, to ourselves, and to another human being the exact nature of our wrongs."

I remember the first time I wrote my inventory. I gave it to my sponsor in front of the fireplace, and we cried. I knew enough to cry because I saw everybody else cry and I thought it was appropriate. What good was an inventory unless you cried? So I cried and I tore up my inventory and threw it into the fireplace.

Then my sponsor said, "Now go write an inventory!" I was trying to impress him with the exact nature of my wrongs. But it was really everybody else's inventory but my own.

Finally, in working on my inventories, I learned that what is important in doing them is seeing where you really are through another's eyes. By sharing my inventory I get to see how others see me — and gradually I get to see myself clearly.

Step Five begins, "Admitted to God, to ourselves, and to another human being . . ." I'll tell you, the hardest part of this step was not admitting my wrongs to God or another human being. The hardest part was admitting them to myself. It was hard to sit down, look myself in the *eye*, and say, "You really are that way, Bill. You do things that hurt other people and yourself." When I looked at my character defects, I thought they weren't really *my* defects, because my mother caused them. I wrote an inventory, but I kept thinking my mother caused my behavior — or my father caused it, or a teacher caused it.

I used to blame a teacher I once had for causing all my problems with grammar. When I went into this teacher's grammar class, my reputation had preceded me, so the teacher said to me, "Oh, I know who you are. You sit in the back of the room and I never want to hear from you again." To this day I still have this tremendous mental block when it comes to grammar. I used to say that I had this mental block *because of the teacher,* and that justified it. Now I say, "The teacher did that, but *I* have the mental block." So what? I could stop having it anytime I wanted to. But it doesn't seem to be a particular hindrance to me, and it would take a lot of effort to learn grammar now. I would rather put the effort into having fun, so I keep the mental block.

The reason Steps Four and Five are separate steps is to help us see ourselves as we really are. For many of us, writing an inventory is bad enough. Sharing it is even more difficult and demeaning. We find it easiest to do it backwards, admitting our wrongs to another person first. Then we admit maybe a little bit to God and very little to ourselves.

People ask me, "Well, can't I make an inventory of the good things, too?" The answer is no. There's plenty of time for that. It's the wrong you want to get rid of. You aren't asking God to rid you of your good qualities. The whole purpose of doing an inventory is to get rid of character defects, not to find reasons for them or to rationalize inappropriate behavior.

Do we really admit our wrongs to ourselves? It's very important to deal with that and be willing to have ourselves appear in our inventories just as we really are. I have to admit to God, to myself, and to another human being the exact nature of *my* wrongs. I do not believe the inventory is an opportunity to divulge others' participation in my wrongs. It is never necessary to name names or break anyone else's anonymity.

People ask, "Does the inventory have to be written?" Nothing *has* to be done in this Program. Nothing says you have to do anything you don't want to do. Though there are reasons for the steps, they are only suggested steps.

One reason for sharing your inventory with another person is that we really cannot appraise ourselves. We need another person to help us see ourselves as we really are. The crux of Step Five is the word *humility.* We often take that word to mean *humiliation,* but what it really means is being humble, being unafraid to share our lives.

If nothing else, our Program of recovery gives us hope. The example set by others shows us that we are not alone, that our deepest, darkest secrets are shared by others. We are not unique in our fears and fantasies, and that is comforting.

From the moment I walked into my first recovery meeting, I was aware of one single thing: I would never again be alone with my problem of compulsive overeating. There were people there from all walks of life who shared their mysteries — and their mysteries were mine.

We have to be honest with another person when we take this Fifth Step. It is important that the person we choose to share our lives with be able to keep a confidence. Giving an inventory is a matter of life and death. The Big Book uses those words because that's how important it is. The person sharing his or her inventory must impress on the person listening that it *is* a matter of life and death; otherwise there's no value to sharing it.

Literally, your life does depend on sharing your inventory. It doesn't mean you're going to die if you don't give away your inventory, but you do choose whether you are going to really *live.* Until you share your inventory, you are not really living, but are "among the walking dead." We can choose to be dead or to live. Before I started following the Program, I was dead. When I found the Program, I fooled around with it for about three years — and then I wasn't dead anymore. I've chosen life by choosing to give away my inventory.

The person you choose to hear your inventory may be anyone whom you trust who can also be objective about the things you share. Some people go to a doctor or a minister. Some people ask their sponsors to hear their inventories, so I'd like to go into sponsorship for a moment here.

In this Program, each person has a sponsor and each of us has the opportunity to be a sponsor to someone else. A sponsor's role is very simple. However, let me say first that I don't believe in food sponsors. I think it is destructive to both of the people involved. My personal belief is that having food sponsors is counter-productive to losing weight and has nothing to do with our Program. Over and over again I see that all a food sponsor does is to allow both the sponsor and the sponsoree to be deluded into thinking that dieting is going to work. It appears to work, but it really doesn't.

I believe a sponsor has only one job, and that is to be supportive of the person he or she sponsors by guiding that person through the steps. That's it. When somebody asks me to deal with a problem, I'll listen and I'll be supportive. But though I may point things out, I don't ever give advice. I'm not there for that. I *am* there to direct others to the steps of the Program. I don't tell anyone to get rid of a spouse or quit a job — that's not for me to say. My sole job as a sponsor is to support you — no matter what you do. Leave your spouse or don't leave . . . it doesn't make any difference as far as I'm concerned. The important thing is to help you stop feeling bad about yourself, to help you stop thinking about rights and wrongs.

I don't deal with rights and wrongs much anymore. I deal only with what works and what doesn't. What you or I did in the past was not wrong — it just didn't work for us. It might have worked for others, but for us it didn't. We need to learn to do what *does* work.

How do you handle listening to someone's inventory? When people want to share their inventories with me, we sit down and read the inventory together. I might say, "That sounds like grandiosity." I don't tell them they *are* this or that; I just suggest what seem to me to be character defects. It's really none of my business what their character defects are. I'm there to listen, I'm there for them to share with.

It's important that they share and it's important that they really face themselves. You can't let them get away with skimming over an inventory. A sponsor is there to help them handle and accept the past, to see that their character defects really do belong to them. They've got to be willing to turn it all over to a Higher Power.

Being a good sponsor is not easy. It is one of the most difficult relationships we can have. It means being a friend — and even more than that. A sponsor must be willing to allow pain to surface. I think we go through life too often denying each other the right to be uncomfortable, to experience pain. There is nothing wrong with being uncomfortable or in feeling upset. What's wrong is what we do about it. Parents often deny their children the right to cry. Kids grow up thinking parents are going to take away all unhappiness and uncomfortableness. But of course parents can't do that. We grow up thinking it's wrong to be in pain and we deny each other the right to have pain as adults.

As a sponsor, I will not cajole people into writing their inventories. When they're ready, they'll do their inventories. If they're not ready, that's their problem. Anytime they're ready to change their lives it's going to work for them.

Once they do write their inventories, people sometimes call me up and say something like "I'd like to give my inventory to you when you have time." But I tell them I don't have time — and that really throws them back. They say, "What do you mean you don't have time? You're always talking about inventories."

I reply, "I'm a very busy person."

"Well," they say, "shall I give it to someone else, then?"

Then I say, "That's up to you."

They are confused and say, "How can I give my inventory to you if you don't have the time?" I tell them to read what the Big Book says about the Fifth Step.

I'm not there to get anybody to do anything. But if someone says, "Listen, Bill, I have to do this. Now you stop and give me the time I want because my life depends upon it," I will say that I have the time and am willing to listen — because that person said his or her life depended upon it. My life depends upon sharing my inventory and you must be willing to accept the fact that your life depends upon it.

You know, some people say that I use poor terminology because I always say that the best way to help people who have fallen down is to kick them. But every time I bend down to help somebody up, I get kicked — and they get nowhere. When I bend down and help somebody up, it's as though I were telling that person, "You know, stupid, you can't get up without my help." Want to know something? They *can* get up without my help. There is nobody in this Program who needs my help directly; I'm there as God's instrument, but I can only help *myself*. I can't cure anybody, I don't want to cure anybody — I want to help me.

By asking someone in the Program to hear your inventory or talk over a problem, you're really giving that person a chance to give away what he or she has learned about working the steps. The sponsor says, "Boy, am I lucky. This person has a problem that I always had. I dealt with it and as I share it, I realize I've grown because I don't have to deal with it so much anymore." And the sponsoree says, "Boy, if that other person can do it, so can I." That's how sponsorship works.

Step Six

"Were entirely ready to have God remove all these defects of character."

I took the words of the Sixth Step literally. It says "were entirely ready" — *ready,* not active, not *doing* something. In Step Six you'll find out that as much as you think you want God to remove all your defects of character, there are lots of them you won't want to give up! You see, giving up our character defects and becoming sane makes us feel very vulnerable. Lots of us would rather have rotten lives than have no life at all. We'd rather have miserable love than have no love. We stay with unhealthy relationships rather than risk having no relationships at all. We keep our lousy feelings rather than risk having no feelings. Even though we seem ready to have God remove our defects of character, we still resist.

For instance, we find it difficult to look at anger and deal with it. It's hard to face up to it, feel it, and not let it explode all over. I used to have two options with anger.

First, I could act it out — maybe even hit someone. Second, I could hold it in. When I was young I hit people, until I found out I could go to jail for that. The rest of my life — until I came into the Program — I held it in, kept it bottled inside of me. I thought those were the only two options I had.

Now I know there is a third option. That is to choose not to be angry. I found out that by just letting the feeling be, it would go away. By either holding it in or lashing out at someone, I used to give anger a lot of power. Anger became a kind of a god. It controlled me because I gave it so much power.

The word "appropriate" is one of my favorite words. It is totally inappropriate for anyone to be insane. It is totally inappropriate for anybody to be fat, to be drunk, or to use dope. We compulsive overeaters are fortunate to the extent that we can see our inappropriateness — our bodies get bigger, our heads get fatter. That's inappropriate for us.

What we really have to do is to be willing to have God remove our mania for food, for anger, for resentment, for guilt, for hostility — one at a time.

I never knew I could literally stop eating. I thought that if I was hungry, I had to eat. If food was in front of me, I had to eat it. I never knew that I could just stop eating.

I was given a simple assignment which helped learn I could stop eating. It worked for me, and I'll pass it on to you. My sponsor asked, "Why do you eat everything on your plate? Leave one string bean."

I said, "That's ridiculous." Hungry or not, I was going to eat it, right?

My sponsor said, "Leave one string bean. Whether you think it's stupid or not, do it."

Okay — so I left one string bean. Let me tell you, that was the hardest thing in the world to do. I had never left anything on my plate before. I mean, I thought I just couldn't leave one string bean. But I did it — I left the one string bean. The next day my sponsor asked what I was having for dinner. I said, "I don't know — meat, salad, vegetable." He said, "Leave one piece of vegetable and leave a little piece of meat today."

That's how it works. You have to force yourself to walk away from food — literally. I left a little something each time, and do you know what? I was no less hungry or more hungry. I didn't lose any more weight or any less weight. It was a symbol, and pretty soon I became more and more comfortable leaving something. What happened is that I learned to pause after each bite and ask myself, "Am I really hungry? Do I really want this?" Eventually I began to realize that I didn't want any more. I really can live without the next bite. To this day I leave something of everything. If I look down at my plate and I haven't left something, I know I'm not working my Program.

How can you do that? Well, you just do it, that's all. Start out with one string bean, one pea, one carrot — one of anything. Just leave it, and build up from there. I can stop right now in the middle of a meal. Am I really hungry? Do I really need this? When I get to a certain point, I can stop. I have been given that power.

That's how it starts out — with one string bean. It's the most practical approach I know for stopping compulsive behavior. It separated me from that little boy inside who said, "I can't do it. I don't want to do it." Each of us has that child inside who says, "I can't do it." Well, as long as we believe we can't do it, we can't. Sometimes we need a little proof. So just take one thing you think you can't do and do it. It will separate you from the little child inside of you, the little child who says, "I can't help myself."

Believe me, the obsession for food is the easiest thing you'll ever get rid of. When I got rid of my food problem, suddenly other things turned up. I had to deal with relationships, honesty, even accepting the weather the way it was. It's as though I had picked up a rock and there was all this other stuff underneath. Sometimes I want to put the rock back.

Life has become increasingly more difficult now that I have to deal with all these other things too. Life for me is kind of like a dike — I'm constantly trying to plug up the hole. Every time I plug one hole, four more show up. When I came to this Program, I had one problem. I was a compulsive overeater, they told me. I thought that meant I was fat, and that all I had to do was go on a diet and lose weight. Everything was then going to be fantastic. I was going to be cured. But that's not so. When I solved the problem of compulsive overeating, I found I had more problems to deal with.

We start out on this program like a young architect whose first job is to build an addition, a room onto a house. This architect practices until he or she can handle this, then is given another job — to do a house, then a hospital, then a city block, then a skyscraper, then a whole town. Our problems do not lessen on this Program; our capacity to deal with them, however, increases infinitely.

Until the obsession for physical self-destruction is removed, you are going to play a game. Some people indulge in binges. Some people keep the weight off but get into other obsessions. You can sit around and say that you've been thin for ten years, but unless the obsession for food is removed, you're going to play the game one way or the other. Obsessive behavior is destructive to me. I cannot go through life obsessed and say that I've recovered. The problem of obsessions will be removed by God when I'm willing to have it removed. I have become the kind of person who lets God remove my problems. I have absolute faith.

I've seen plenty of people stop overeating or stop drinking — and they have nothing except that they've stopped. Certainly, it is an achievement to have stopped overeating or drinking, but there's more to life than that. A person who stops overeating or drinking but doesn't fill up his or her life with the steps of the Program is still crippled, not recovered. A truly happy person is free — free from anger, depression, and fear. We have to deal with the character defects that compulsive overeating covers up.

I really believe that you are never the same once you start the Program. Sometimes I would really like to be back in my old insanity. Life was very simple then. I could explain everything. I was fat and my mother caused it. If the traffic was bad and I got a ticket, it was because I was fat and my mother caused it. If I got divorced, it was because I was fat and my mother caused it. Whatever happened, I could explain it very simply.

I can't do that now. I have to sit back and say, "You know what? I got a ticket today and it was my fault. I acted the way I did because I have a character defect that I refuse to allow God to remove." If I keep trying to cure myself of this character defect, there's no way I'm going to get rid of it. The Program says, "Why don't you just let go and let God take care of it?"

I was never "ready" to lose weight. I thought I was, but I wasn't really *willing.* Sometimes we excuse ourselves from moving on by saying, "I don't have a good grasp on life." How do you know if you have a good grasp? Will a bolt from heaven come down to let you know? If you can just be *willing* to change, you have a good enough grasp on life.

There is another concept that is a crucial part of the Program. We have to understand that there is nothing *we* can do about our character defects and we have to understand what we really mean when we say this. When somebody I sponsor comes up to me and says, "I've got this terrible resentment and I keep doing this. What can I do about it?" I say, "Nothing." If we adapt the Big Book for us compulsive overeaters, it says we are compulsive overeaters and cannot manage our own lives, that probably no human power can relieve our compulsive overeating. Do you get that? *No human power can relieve our compulsive overeating.* There is no way you can stop compulsively overeating, lying, being afraid, being angry, being depressed, or whatever. You might as well stop trying to do anything about it.

I used to think the way to get rid of resentment was to look at how bad I was for having that resentment. Then I'd go to somebody I resented and apologize. They'd say, "Well, it's about time you came around." Then I was even more resentful. I had not yet let go of that character defect, and no matter what I did, it was there.

I spent all my life trying to change me. First it was, "Hold in your anger." Then it was, "No, let out your anger. Don't show your resentment." And then, "Be honest about your resentment." I've worked on resentments, anger, and depression, and I've worked on compulsive overeating. I tried to get rid of all of those things — and sometimes for short periods of time I seemed to succeed. But all along there has been nothing I could do to get rid of any one of these defects. I always found another one to replace it or else I took it back.

The more we are willing to allow God to remove our character defects, the more he removes them. That's what it means to turn them over to God. Does that mean we sit back and say, "Okay, God, I've got anger. You take it?" To me it means exactly that. Does He always take it away? Always. My character defects are always taken away *to the degree that I'm willing to allow them to be taken away.* The problem is that I am often not willing. It's one thing to say I don't want to be angry anymore, but it's another thing to realize that I really like being angry sometimes. That's especially true when I feel justified and can be righteous about it.

I used to like depression. People would ask, "What's the matter, Bill? You look so down." I got a lot of attention from that. I hid behind it. I used my character defects, as we all do, to explain lots of things, especially to explain not feeling good about myself.

Next time someone says you're sloppy, say, "You're right, and there's nothing I can do about it. It's a character defect of mine. There's nothing I can do except allow God to remove it from me. I'm willing to allow God to remove it." What you're going to find out is that all of a sudden you will have a sense of pride from doing things differently. Of course God will remove those defects. Just think — I just saved you a lifetime of working at all those character defects. All you have to do is sit back and say, "There is nothing I can do about them except to be willing to have them be removed."

I used to say, "Well, I can't have God remove *all* these defects of character." It was just another rationalization. I thought I could never be perfect, so I rationalized that I didn't need to try at all. I refused to allow God to remove my problems.

So Step Six is the part of the Program in which we see our character defects and recognize the effect they have on our lives and the lives of all those we touch. We must become willing to live without the negative excitement of feeling bad and the consequences of that excitement, or we will destroy ourselves and those around us — who are usually the ones we love the most. Willingness is the key, as the *Twelve Steps and Twelve Traditions* suggests. And trust is the pathway.

Step Seven

"Humbly asked Him to remove our shortcomings."

This step deals with the problem of humility. The desire to seek and do God's will — which is a large part of humility — has been missing in most of us. It was certainly missing in me.

One defect which kept me from gaining humility was self-centered fear. Fear is one of our biggest enemies. Some people say we need "good fear." To me there's no such thing as "good fear" in my life. I don't want to be afraid of anything. I'm no longer afraid of food or of people, places, or things. I've filled up my life with feelings other than fear.

The chapter on Step Seven (p. 76) in *Twelve Steps and Twelve Traditions* reminds us that if humility could enable us to find the grace which banished our greatest obsession, then there must be hope that humility will also help us remove any other problem we could possibly have. We *can* banish problems — if we have humility.

Humility is difficult to achieve. It doesn't require groveling. It doesn't mean making yourself *less*. Having humility means being honest — being what you really are. In so doing, you become *more* than you used to be.

To have God remove our shortcomings means to offer ourselves to God. We let go of our shortcomings by saying, "God, I offer myself to you to do with me as you wish." Letting go means that we don't have to do anything about our shortcomings anymore. Just by offering ourselves to God, our shortcomings are removed.

When these things are removed, a void is left inside us. We start out having good feelings and bad feelings. As our shortcomings are removed, we have fewer and fewer bad feelings, but if the good feelings don't increase to fill in the emptiness, there's just a void there. Many of us experience that feeling of emptiness after we lose weight. We feel like saying, "Is that it?" Life doesn't feel full or exciting enough. We're used to being filled up with all those bad feelings.

So we set ourselves up deliberately to sabotage ourselves. We start out with a relationship or a job and we find a way to mess it up to make it exciting. We don't want to be overlooked; we want everything really lively. When we mess things up, everybody gets excited. We don't want to get rid of the excitement of those times when people tell us how bad we are.

One particular character defect I had for many years caused me a lot of anxiety. I felt guilty about it and said to myself, "You shouldn't have this problem, especially after being on the Program. With all this educational background, you shouldn't be doing what you're doing. There's no reason for you to do it." I really laid a trip on myself. But I continued to have the character defect. Finally one day I looked at myself and said, "What a jerk you are! Obviously you're going to keep doing this. You've got this character defect and you're not willing to stop. So why don't you stop beating yourself over the head and accept the fact that you're a real jerk. That's it."

I'm telling you, it had been such a load to carry. But as soon as I realized what I was doing to myself, the load was gone, because it didn't serve any purpose anymore. I became willing to have God remove the character defect from me.

We can't accomplish much unless we take hold of those character defects, set them down, and say, "That's it. Those defects are me. I own them. Nobody made me this way." Oh, we can say "My mother did this" or "My father did that." They may have initiated resentment in us, but they aren't causing it now. We are grown people. We need to assume responsibility for our present state of being. We need to say to ourselves "I am what I am. These are my character defects," and "God, I don't want them any more." It's very simple.

One prayer in the Big Book asks God to take away my character defects so that I can serve God and other people — not so that I will feel better, not so that I will lose weight or be thin, but so that I can serve God and my fellows better. The prayer asks God to grant us strength to do what God asks of us. Only then, according to the Big Book, have we completed Step Seven.

The purpose of Steps Six and Seven is to help you see your character defects and allow God to remove them. Look at all the years you've spent trying to straighten yourself out. All that time you've been running around saying, "Isn't it terrible I've got this . . . Isn't it terrible I've got that . . . What can I do?" The answer is: allow God to remove whatever it is that troubles you. That separates the believers from the nonbelievers because it's very difficult to stand there and say, "You mean to tell me that if I go around spitting on sidewalks and getting tickets for it all the time and I can't stop, if I ask God to remove *that* defect, He will?"

That's right. That's exactly the way it works. As a matter of fact, it has never worked any other way for me. I tried all my life to straighten myself out, but all I did was become more sophisticated in how *not* to straighten out. I tried to twist everything my way. It didn't work. I kept going out there and saying, "One more diet, one more inspiration — then I will be willing, and I'll do it." But there's actually nothing to *do*.

Many people come into the Program after a lot of therapy. They have an advantage because at least they're open and aware. They can see their character defects. But even though it is important to see our character defects, we have to remember that we don't have to do anything about them anymore. We don't have to worry about overeating or anything else.

Overeaters, talking about food, always ask, "How do you keep from overeating? How do you accomplish abstinence?" I tell them that if you do what the Program tells you to do — follow the steps — abstinence will come automatically.

The Program also helps us see that we carry out inappropriate feelings in inappropriate ways, or carry out appropriate feelings in inappropriate ways. For instance, we eat when we're not hungry or feel hungry when we've just eaten. Some people are hungry all the time and that's inappropriate. Eating the way we eat — or the reverse, anorexia, not eating or eating and throwing up — it's all the same thing: inappropriate.

When I want to eat, when I have that compulsion, I'm going to eat. When I have a compulsion to be angry, I'm going to be angry. When I have a compulsion to drive my car at seventy miles an hour the wrong way on a one-way street, then I'm going to do it. When I have a compulsion to manipulate and control, then I'm going to do that.

How can you stop a certain kind of behavior when you have a compulsion to do it? The Program tells us that God will do for us what we have never been able to do for ourselves. If you can tell me an easier way, I'll do it. That's why taking each step in the Program — in order — is so important. Each step allows us to move toward learning to have faith. The Program is perfectly planned that way. You have to understand where the Program starts and where it's going.

There are some character defects that I have never seen anybody get rid of by *trying* to get rid of them. I've seen people with these defects become more sophisticated — like the alcoholic who goes around losing his job, going to jail, and driving recklessly. Or the man who says, "Well, I used to lie and I don't lie anymore." Sure, he doesn't lie anymore, but now he withholds his feelings and he's eating himself up inside. He's dying. Very often, people channel the underlying causes of their compulsions into other compulsions. A dry alcoholic might be out of a job all the time, using the excuse that he or she has a lot of anger. We have to deal with the underlying causes of our character defects.

It really is an incredible load off my mind to know that I don't have to cure myself of a defect of character. There is nothing I can do. God will take care of it for me. The more I tried to get rid of my character defects, the more I indulged in them. It really is a wonderful relief not to have to go through that anymore.

One very dangerous thing we can do to people who compulsively overeat is to take away their compulsive eating without helping them find any replacement for that behavior. Unless there is a ready replacement, what's going to fill up their lives? They will feel dead. That's why we have things we *do* in the Program — we work the steps, we tell others about the Program, we become sponsors.

The big problem with people who have been in the Program a long time is that we become complacent. We say, "Well, I've been speaking to groups for years. How many times can I speak?" The answer is that there is no limit. It's the same with sponsorship — I sponsor three people or thirty, depending on my ability to serve. There's no limit. How many of us really go out and help compulsive overeaters out there? How often do we serve them — and others?

My experience is that my character defects come back whenever I'm unwilling to work the Program. When I see them coming back, I start getting desires for food. I don't look for someone to blame or a reason for my behavior. Instead I say, "How come I'm not working the Program?" And then I have to accelerate.

We have emphasized that willingness is indispensable. Are we now ready to let God remove from us all the things which we have admitted are objectionable? Can He now take them all? If not — if we cling to something and will not let it go, then we must ask God to help us to be willing.

When we are ready, we can say something like this prayer from the Big Book: "My Creator, I am now willing that you should have all of me, good and bad. I pray that you now remove from me every single defect of character which stands in the way of my usefulness to you and my fellows. Grant me strength, as I go out from here, to do your bidding. Amen" (p. 76).

You have then completed Step Seven. Do you understand now what it's telling you? Just remember what it says. We approach this Program without qualifications. We say, "God, do with me as you would." What I'm really asking is that all my defects be removed. I compulsively eat, I don't always pay my traffic tickets, I don't always answer phone calls, and sometimes I drive my car too fast. Why do I do these things? I do them in order to feel bad.

I used to get in elevators and look at people and think, "I wish I were a real person. Those are real people in the elevator. I'm just a nothing." Now I get into elevators, I look around, I stand up straight, people look at me and smile. I smile back. I know I'm worthy now. It's not through anything I've done except work a spiritual program. It all came automatically.

Sometimes I've asked God to stop an activity of mine and it hasn't stopped. What has happened, though, is that I don't feel bad about it anymore. Then I ask myself why I'm doing it if I don't feel bad about it. I begin to see that behavior for what it is. We're programmed to feel bad — but we must program ourselves to feel good.

I know how well I'm working my Program when I get into my car in the morning. I know how I am each day not by how I eat, but by how I drive my car. I used to love to go to my office. I have to drive over the mountains of Los Angeles and I'd go around those mountains as though I were racing in the Grand Prix. Now when I get up to the top of the mountains and start driving too fast, I pull over to the side and give myself about three minutes. I tell myself to calm down and I ask God to remove that urge.

What God did was remove my desire. If you have a $20,000 sportscar and you're going twenty-five miles per hour around curves, you might as well get rid of the car. That's what I had to do. You see, it wasn't any fun anymore having that car and driving slowly. I got rid of it because the desire was gone.

I used to be totally obsessive. Every minute of my waking hours I was obsessed with something. Now there are many times that I am not obsessed, even though there *are* many times that I do crazy things. I think part of the reason is that I have to eat to survive. This means that every day I engage in the very activity that is symbolic of my obsession — eating. I think every one of us engages in crazy activities during a given day. We do things in an insane manner — out of compulsion. Some of these are very minor. But in the past whenever I engaged in obsessive behavior, I felt bad about it. I ate over feeling bad. Then I felt bad over eating. Now I can do something crazy and recognize it for what it is — but I don't have to feel bad about it.

If we only talk about our obsessions and about having them removed, we can't really be of maximum service to God and the people about us. The whole idea behind the Twelve Steps is to create the kind of person who can be of service to other people and to God. I can't be of service if I'm self-obsessed, if I'm destroying myself.

If you didn't have your character defects to talk about, what would you talk about? Do you know how to talk about good times? How long would your conversation be? So many people are used to complaining about life that they don't know how to talk about anything else. One person says, "You know, I went to the beach Sunday and I want to share how joyous it was." The other person says, "Oh yeah, that's very nice. Let me tell you about my ulcer."

We do that at home — it's typical in relationships. A man walks into his house and asks his wife how her day was. She says, "Oh, the mortgage is overdue, the kid failed at school, the meat I bought today is rotten, and we have no dinner." She asks her husband how things went for him. He says, "Oh, I got a raise today at work, but I had a flat tire. The work is too much anyway." We don't say, "I feel great. I had a terrific day." Life seems to have no meaning for us unless we complain.

Try making a commitment for a day — just one day. Say to yourself, "I'm not going to complain about anything, no matter what. I'm not going to use any words except 'okay' if somebody asks how I feel." You will feel like you're going crazy. But you're really going sane. It may feel very uncomfortable, because most people around us are crazy! It's uncomfortable to be around crazy people when you're going sane.

God will remove your defects of character — and you'd better watch out. For every one removed, ten more will show up. What happens is that when we start living this Program, it works terrifically for us. We are relieved of the compulsion to overeat, just as God promised us. Now we can work on other things.

Steps Eight and Nine

"Made a list of all persons we had harmed and became willing to make amends to them all."

"Made direct amends to such people whenever possible, except when to do so would injure them or others."

Making a list of persons we have harmed is so difficult for us — and so important! We cannot work this Program until — as *Twelve Steps and Twelve Traditions* says — we develop the best possible relations with every human being we know.

The process of making amends is broken into two steps. First, in Step Eight, we must be ready to sit down and make our lists of persons we have harmed. Then in Step Nine we determine just how to make amends — and we go out and do it. What is most essential is our *willingness* to make those amends.

Harm is defined practically in *Twelve Steps and Twelve Traditions* as "the result of instincts in collision, which cause physical, mental, emotional, or spiritual damage to people" (p. 80). While we don't *cause* others to act a certain way (they always have a choice in how they react), still everything we do brings forth a response from those around us. If we are bad-tempered, we can expect others to be angry, too. If we are dishonest, others will not trust us. In a thousand ways, we deprive people of emotional or economic security, peace of mind, even property. We can be controlling, neglectful, conniving, thieving, impatient, grandiose, or self-pitying. Start from here and add your own adjectives.

Now is the time — in Steps Eight and Nine — to make amends to right our relationships.

There are those who tell me that they don't have any amends to make, or perhaps only one or two minor situations to rectify. But in my experience a day does not go by that I don't have some amends to make. The list is exhaustive, page after page, derived from my Fourth Step inventory. It includes everyone I ever harmed, thought of harming, or imagined I had harmed.

Occasionally, you'll hear an alcoholic claim that all he or she needs to do is keep sober. Or a compulsive overeater will say that the only thing he or she needs to do it keep "abstinent" (limit themselves to suggested kinds of foods).Sobriety for the alcoholic, or "abstinence" for the compulsive overeater does, of course, become an important part of their lives.

But more is needed than just keeping sober or keeping "abstinent." These compulsive people — after years of insensitive behavior which tried the love and patience of mothers, wives, husbands, and children — have plenty of restitutions to make.

For, as the Big Book says on page 82, "The alcoholic is like a tornado roaring his way through the lives of others. Hearts are broken. Sweet relationships are dead. Affections have been uprooted. Selfish and inconsiderate habits have kept the home in turmoil." The same can be said about the compulsive overeater. A compulsive person is unthinking to believe that sobriety or "abstinence," by itself, is enough.

Most of us are at least willing to make a beginning, to draw up a list of those we have harmed. The best place to find that list is to go back to our Fourth Step inventories and the people we mentioned in it.

My list goes back in time to my childhood, to age three in fact. I can remember harming my house-keeper, my older sister, my parents.

I was five when my younger sister was born and I harmed a cousin by persuading him to run away from home. No incident is too far back to consider.

This is a Program of change. And you cannot change yourself by blaming others, or complaining that your mother did this or your father did that. You can only change *you*, and in order to change, the wreckages of the past must be cleared up.

Isn't it interesting that Step Nine is the first step in which we deal with other people? Until now, the steps concerned only ourselves. Now, perhaps for the first time in our lives, we serve other people by going to them to make amends.

Many of us refuse to take this step or put it off. I don't like looking someone in the eye and saying, "You know, I lied to you." The disappointment on that person's face and my total embarrassment is not only uncomfortable, but humbling. Still, I know I have to do it. We compulsive overeaters eat because of our own unatoned wrongs to others. It is time to get rid of the guilt.

I remember living in a town where I had to pass by a five-and-dime store on the way to school. A group of us would walk in the back door and out the front, stealing as we went. Not long ago, I went back to that store, found the manager, told him my story, and wrote out a check that I figured would cover the candy I had stolen. As I explained why I was doing this, he could not believe it. He himself was considerably overweight, so I talked to him about the Program.

Afterwards I got a letter from the store owners, who wanted to make a donation to Overeaters Anonymous, which, of course, does not accept donations. Since this was not possible, they then asked if they could make a donation to a charity of my choice, because they had never heard of anyone returning so many years afterwards to make good a bad situation.

So I believe we do need to go back in time, to make every effort to seek out people we have harmed. Even after years of searching, I still have not been able to track down some people I went to school with at age ten or eleven. Every time I go to a new city, I look up those old names in the hotel phone book, just on the chance that I might find them. While I'm undertaking this search, I feel terrific about it!

A young girl I sponsored traveled five hundred miles to a town where she had once lived, in order to make amends to some of her girlfriends from school days for stealing their boyfriends. She felt she *had* to do this.

Others have returned to places where they were formerly employed and confessed that they stole money and would like to pay it back. Sometimes the employers do not accept it. Sometimes they are rude or, understandably, angry. The point is not to make these people feel good about us or to win their trust; it is to unburden ourselves of guilt and earn back our own regard for ourselves.

Don't expect forgiveness as you take this step. Your life does not depend upon others' forgiveness, but upon *your* willingness to forgive *you*. No matter what terrible, dark deed you may have done to somebody, someone else among us has also done it or worse. The darkest deed of all is not to forgive yourself.

Don't even expect your family to forgive you. Lots of family members won't. We know that we have driven away many a husband, wife, child, or parent. Some of us have stepped on so many toes and hurt so many people and, in some cases, destroyed lives that we are never going to be forgiven. But there are others out there who are willing to love you, to be with you. As you change and get thin and become a different person, you can't just look at the past, you have to look at the future.

If others want to hang on to rancor and resentment, that is their choice. But *you* don't have to live with guilt — that hallmark of the compulsive overeater — anymore. Perhaps normal people can afford to live with guilt, but for us compulsive types, it is, as the Big

Book says, poison. Some of us find guilt so delicious that we wallow in it and refuse to give it up. If we did give it up, then we would have to allow ourselves to be happy and get on with the business of living! For me, as I work this Program, guilt is no longer a part of my existence.

In reality, I am not working this step for other people. This is a step for me. Whether or not people are willing to accept my amends is of no real consequence to me; they may choose to forgive me or not.

I have a sister whom I haven't talked with for many years, because I was once a person who did things she refused to accept. She is still thinking I'm back there where I was. I don't blame her — or anyone else who knew me in those days — for not forgiving me. We can't blame those who don't forgive us for past wrongs, even though we feel that they are missing out on knowing the people we have become.

Step Nine says, "Made direct amends to those people whenever possible, *except when to do so would injure them or others.*" The Big Book says we cannot buy our peace of mind at the expense of others. In other words, we cannot dump our true confessions on other people and upset their lives.

It is tempting to want to pass the hot potatoes. For instance, two friends of mine were divorced because one woman, attempting to make amends, told the wife about an incident involving her husband, then walked away. Her "amends" destroyed the marriage. Prudence dictates that we not unload ourselves at the risk of harming others. Also, we need not steep ourselves in excessive remorse before those we have harmed. We just go to them straight without arguing or criticizing, tell them what our wrong was, and deal with the consequences of our conduct.

You will have problems doing this; you will fight it. You may be worried enough about it to want to skip the Ninth Step altogether. Can you skip this step? Sure, you can, but when you begin to put on weight and binge after peeling off one hundred pounds or so, you may not have to wonder why!

If you like yourself, you will make amends, even when those you approach are rude or crass or say, "It's about time!" You will know that for a day, for a week, for an hour, you will be free from compulsion — from insanity — because you took that step. You make amends, not for what you are going to get from the person you have harmed, not from any motive at all except that you want to be of maximum service to God and man. You can be of service only if you are free from those past wreckages.

I think that this step does not really work until you are hurting enough. Then you're going to say, "Maybe this whole procedure is ridiculous, but what else is there for me? I'm going to give it a try. I'm going to work at it!"

The Big Book gives us some guidelines for those who might have committed a criminal offense which could lead to jail if it were known to the authorities. On page 79 it cites as an example the story of a man who had remarried, who would have been sent to prison if he had confessed his past wrongs. If a person is certain to be prosecuted and jailed, and therefore would be unable to earn a living for his family, then those needs must be considered. There are ways, in a case like this, to make amends anonymously.

As for our forgiving others — I find it easy to forgive anyone because I can forgive by worshiping. I don't forgive a person's conduct, but there is God in everybody and I can worship God in that person.

I can't forgive my mother's conduct, but I can worship the God in her and appreciate the good things that we had and the fact that she, as I did, had an insanity, although she expressed it in a different way.

If someone is really angry or nasty, I make a concerted effort to find the little part of that person that is God — and that is what I concentrate on. The God part is what I am going to deal with.

In this Program, our primary goal is not to lose weight or to become sober, but to find the spiritual experience. We ask that we be given the strength and direction to do the right thing, to make our amends, no matter what the consequences to us may be — even losing our jobs or our reputations. *We have to be willing.*

As you work this Program, you will discover that the person you were, the unhappy child inside you will die. (I'm talking about that old childhood message that tells you you're no good). That image of youself should have faded away long ago. You may have trouble letting go of that image; you may feel sad, maybe even a little lonely without it. But thank God you never again have to be the person you once were!

Compulsive overeating is the acting out of "I want what I want when I want it." So is drinking and every other compulsive activity. When I want something, I WANT it, and I can't stop wanting it.

The kind of person that has such wants is a child. As a four-year-old child who stamps and screams, "I want it, I want it," and creates a fuss until those wants are satisfied, the compulsive person behaves the same way — whether "it" is really what is wanted or the attention that is generated by the fuss.

In the Big Book story "He Who Loses His Life" on page 534, the man relating his experiences quotes from a poem by Edna St. Vincent Millay:

> *Pity me the heart that is slow to learn*
> *What the quick mind sees at every turn.*

What this couplet illustrates is that the intellect is more mature than the emotions. Intellect sees, but emotions still act out. The man in the Big Book story has a definition of alcoholism which applies also to compulsive overeating; it is "a state of being in which the emotions have failed to grow to the stature of the intellect" (p. 535).

As the person with "the grown-up brain and the childish emotions" grows older, such traits as "vanity, self-interest, false pride, jealousy, longing for social approval" make him or her a likely candidate for alcoholism or compulsive overeating.

So here is the compulsive person at age twenty, thirty, forty, or fifty, with prepuberty emotions. As that person grows older, the gap between intellectual and emotional development becomes so much more painful that he or she abuses alcohol or overeats or creates some other anxiety just to numb the pain.

To adapt for overeaters a statement from the Big Book on page 535: There are some compulsive overeaters who seem to be mature, but the strain of trying to appear grown up causes them to eat compulsively. Such compulsive behavior is "compensation for immaturity," compensation, I believe, for a feeling of inadequacy, a childish vanity.

What the Twelve Step Program does is to allow us to grow up, to give us a second chance at life. Bill W. and this Program have given us the gift of a chance to grow again, to relive our lives. The Program is the synthesis of all the good, positive philosophy we have ever read — all based on love. There is only one law — love. And there are only two sins: to interfere with the growth of another human being and to interfere with one's own growth.

The Big Book says, "The spiritual life is not a theory. *We have to live it*" (p. 83). If we do work at having our defects removed, and at making amends to other people, we CAN find new freedom and new happiness, as well as serenity and peace of mind. The Program promises that our self-pity will vanish, we will develop a new interest in others, our fears will disappear, and we will be able to cope with situations that once confused us.

If we are thorough about these steps, the Big Book tells us that "we will suddenly realize that God is doing for us what we could not do for ourselves" (p. 84).

Step Ten

"Continued to take personal inventory and when we were wrong, promptly admitted it."

I have found that, for me, it's really important to continue to take a personal inventory. I take a steno pad and write on the right side what's bothering me or what I have done that day. I write it down without thinking too much about it. If I start thinking about it, I edit. I want it all to come out unedited.

Then on the left side I write down my corresponding defects of character. In other words, I may write on the right side: "That person did this or that to me." And on the left side I write what it is about me that seemed to bring on his or her behavior.

Then I go back to Step Nine. If I created anxiety for someone, I contact that person and acknowledge my actions. I may say, "I am responsible for a situation today that you saw fit to be angry about, and I apologize." Once I made amends to somebody, not because I went out and deliberately hurt him, but because I created an environment in which he was unhappy and had animosity towards me. I wrote him a ten-page, typewritten letter outlining our relationship as I saw it. The result was that he no longer likes either me or my Program. However, he is entitled to his dislike. I didn't need or expect affirmation, since I was acting for my own benefit primarily.

I make mistakes all the time. It's not wrong to make mistakes, but it is wrong not to learn from them.

A key word in this step is "promptly." I take my continuing inventory and I make amends promptly. This does not mean waiting a week or two, or until I feel more comfortable or ready. If I waited to be "ready," I would still be out there seventy-five pounds heavier.

Putting off making amends allows those old, destructive feelings to come back to me. If I begin to feel bad about myself again, I may need months to undo the self-damage. Although I may be sorry for the way I acted, I don't apologize for my existence anymore. I used to love to feel bad. Now every time I feel that way, I get rid of the feeling.

I never tell myself that I am a "bad person" who should not have done something. Instead I say, "That didn't work." The Big Book tells me that I will know intuitively what works and what doesn't work for me. In making amends to another person, I acknowledge what I did and what effect it had on that person and that I know "it didn't work."

The Tenth Step is a combination of all the preceding steps because it seems to be the first time in our step-by-step progress that we recapitulate. We take all the progress of the first nine steps and begin to apply it to our daily living. As its application becomes more and more automatic, the necessity of the day-by-day or moment-by-moment inventory lessens.

One man I know has insisted for years that the Tenth Step is a useless step. If you are really living your Program and are honest about it, he says, this step becomes automatic. He assumes that we don't have to keep on making lists of people we have harmed today because we wouldn't harm anyone now, and if we did, we would turn around immediately and say, "Excuse me." I do try to make amends immediately. If I find myself in the midst of an old pattern, I say, "Just a second . . . I want to apologize. I should not be saying — or doing — that."

The point of the continuing inventory is to set right these mistakes as we go along. It is a constant, lifelong process.

After this housecleaning, through trust in God the promise of the Program begins to come true. No longer must I worry about food. God literally has taken away my desire for it. God has given me the ability to say, "No, thank you, I really don't care for that food anymore. I have no taste for it."

No longer are we ruled by our character defects. We are hardly aware that we are developing new attitudes. Courtesy and kindness, all of a sudden, become commonplace with us. Tolerance and love for those around us take on new meanings as we no longer react to other people with anger, withdrawal, or the ultimate act of eating compulsively. How can we be intolerant of others, after we recognize that they have tolerated our own sick and insane activities?

As the Program promises, we do begin to react sanely and normally. After all, a sick person who is sane will not engage in an activity that will destroy his or her life. If a doctor tells you not to run because it may kill you, a sane and normal way to react is to follow the doctor's instructions and walk, not run. If you have diabetes and cannot eat certain foods and must take medications, the sane and normal way to react is not to eat those foods and to take your medication, or you will die. By contrast, a person who is insane and unable to react normally because he or she is compulsive cannot, even under threat of death or disability, follow the doctor's orders.

We compulsive overeaters have lost the power of sanity and normality. But when we really live this Program, we do recover. We take the greatest strides in our recovery when the Tenth Step becomes more and more automatic, when self-analysis replaces self-deception and we see our faults and recover from them.

Reacting sanely and normally means to me that, as a person who has a propensity for being fat, I do not eat certain foods, nor do I eat certain quantities of foods. It's not important at all *why* I can't. For me, it is a fact of life.

Now, by following the precepts of the Tenth Step, I have the ability to follow what I know is an essential way of life for me. I have the power of choice. Instead of saying that I cannot eat something because it is not good for me or it is fattening, I can say that I honestly don't want it anymore. The obsession has been removed automatically. I don't feel that it is egotistical now to say that I am sane. It is a fact. Sometimes I do things that are inappropriate, but basically my life has become sane.

Such sane and normal behavior can come only from a Higher Power, because with my own power I was never able to obtain sanity or normality.

I came to this Program powerless. I don't know if I was born that way or not. It really doesn't matter. I do know that every time I try to exercise my own power over food I show a lack of faith and trust in God. If God will do it for me by giving me His power to react sanely and normally, then I no longer need to fight for that ability. I will no longer deny God the right to perform a miracle through me and for me.

As for going back to the way I was, once I have started this Program, I would find it horrible to backtrack. If it was bad being fat in the beginning, imagine losing all that weight and then putting it back on! I would feel ten times as bad, because I have had that vision of freedom and what life is all about.

We have two options: to be sane or to be crazy. And being crazy *again* after we have had a glimpse of what sanity is, is crazier than being crazy in the first place, when we either didn't recognize it or didn't admit it.

I always had a taste for certain foods and was unable to stop eating. Now a miracle has taken place. God has removed the compulsion, the taste, the appetite. This is hard to believe, but true. And this will continue on a daily basis, as long as I follow the Tenth Step and the spiritual path set before me. If I can work this Program, I will always live sanely and normally.

Step Eleven

"Sought through prayer and meditation to improve our conscious contact with God, as we understood Him, praying only for knowledge of His will for us and the power to carry that out."

When people ask me what I pray for, I reply, "The Big Book is my guide." It says to pray "for knowledge of God's will for me and the power to carry it out." So I ask God for His will — that is my prayer. The meditation of Step Eleven is listening to God, for His direction, His will.

Both prayer and meditation are key elements in my conscious communication with God. Prayer is a spiritual tool that enables me to ask for God's will and the power to carry it out. Meditation is a process that helps me prepare myself to receive the word of God. I've learned to pray to God — simply and clearly — for knowledge of His will. I pray for that and nothing more, trying to resist the temptation to pray for my own will and specifics — "Give me this"; "Don't let that happen"; Let me be on time"; "I hope the sun shines tomorrow." Instead I say, "God, show me Your will," and ask for the power, the calmness, and the serenity to carry out that will and effectively deal with the situations in my life.

Hundreds of times each day, I face a fork in the road for me and I can decide to go with God's will or against. I can go ahead and take someone's parking space or let him have it; I can honk and curse at someone who drives slowly or not; I can get angry at a co-worker about an error made or calmly discuss it. By working the Eleventh Step, we can get real insight about God's will for us, along with the power to carry out that will in our lives. We really can have a dynamic, positive relationship with our God; that is what this Program is all about. He communicates His will and we act on that will with our God-given power.

So often I hear people say, "Well, I'm just sitting back. If God wanted me to have a job, I'd have a job. If God wanted me to lose weight, I'd lose weight. If God wanted me to have abstinence, I'd have abstinence." They just sit back and say, "Come on, God, work." Essentially, we are alone in this world with our God. We must learn to recognize our relationship with Him and grow in it. For instance, when you're driving alone late at night and come to a doughnut shop, virtually nothing will keep you from stopping — nothing, that is, except God's will and your power to act on it. The greatest sponsor or the best speaker or the most memorable words of wisdom from a friend will not stop you at that point, from entering the doughnut shop. Only you and your God working together can do that. As compulsive overeaters, at least some areas of our lives have been sorely lacking in discipline. Working the Twelve Steps, along with this daily practice of spiritual communication will bring both discipline and action back into our lives.

The Big Book says it best about prayer on pages 87 and 88: "As we go through the day we pause, when agitated or doubtful, and ask for the right thought or action. We constantly remind ourselves we are no longer running the show, humbly saying to ourselves many times each day, 'Thy will be done.' We are then in much less danger of excitement, fear, anger, worry, self-pity, or foolish decisions. We become much more efficient. We do not tire so easily, for we are not burning up energy foolishly as we did when we were trying to arrange life to suit ourselves."

The prayer of St. Francis of Assisi as it is presented in *Twelve Steps and Twelve Traditions* is a powerful one for me. I say it several times each day:

> *Lord, make me a channel of thy peace —*
> *that where there is hatred, I may bring love*
> *— that where there is wrong, I may bring the*
> *spirit of forgiveness — that where there is*
> *discord, I may bring harmony — that where*
> *there is error, I may bring truth — that where*
> *there is doubt, I may bring faith — that where*
> *there is despair, I may bring hope — that*
> *where there are shadows, I may bring light*
> *— that where there is sadness, I may bring*
> *joy. Lord, grant that I may seek rather to*
> *comfort than to be comforted — to under-*
> *stand, than to be understood — to love, than*
> *to be loved. For it is by self-forgetting that*

*one finds. It is by forgiving that one is
forgiven. It is by dying that one awakens to
Eternal Life. Amen.*

People sometimes tell me that they've prayed but
haven't received an answer from God. I reply that they
can't really be *listening.* We *always* get an answer,
some communication of His will for us.

Life presents us with many decision points or forks
in the road, and we must continually choose which
way to go, which way to respond — negatively,
according to our old compulsive habits or positively,
according to the alternative behavior discovered
through God's will. Without a doubt, God's will is the
right way for our lives.

Meditation is associated with a quiet and intense
thought process. But it has much broader application
when we use it to communicate with our Higher
Power. The Big Book says that meditation is a way of
becoming a channel for communication from our
Higher Power. We need to clear our minds for
listening to and really *hearing* that spiritual communication. And this takes work. When I first started
meditating, I thought I was listening to God, I really
did. The messages that came gave me no spiritual
direction, so I reconsidered my technique. It didn't
take long to discover that I'd been listening to myself
and not God. What was coming through — loud and
clear and in great volume — were voices and messages from my own mind, the shoulds and shouldn'ts
of my values and others, remnants of a daily life filled
with information. I had to learn to become a vessel,

free and clear of any obstruction, in order to receive the word of God.

To those they teach, Zen Masters give a beautiful, hand-painted bowl. Legend is shared that this bowl is centuries old and was painstakingly crafted by a family. The bowl is presented with the question: "What is most valuable about this bowl?" For those who understand, the answer is not its age, its beauty or the legend attached to it, but its capacity to hold. That concept applies to us mortals. What is the most valuable attribute of a human being? Not age, physical appearance or wealth, but the capacity to take information, hold it, and utilize it.

Self-hypnosis has been called a form of meditation. I don't agree. To me self-hypnosis is just substituting one kind of thought process for another. Meditation, on the other hand, is allowing oneself to become like an empty vessel. Only when we're empty can we receive something. We can't take in a thing if we're filled with thoughts of "What am I going to do? How do I look? What should I eat? What should I do here? and What's it going to be like when I get home?"

There are many ways to meditate effectively. Instead of providing an overview of meditation methods, I usually prefer to share my own technique. All I really know about it is that it works for me. It neutralizes my surroundings and helps me get to a level where I can be in conscious contact with God. If possible, I lie down or sit in a chair. I begin by systematically relaxing each part of my body and consciously letting go of the tensions and stiffness I feel. Then, with my body relaxed, I work on clearing my mind. I think carefully about the most peaceful, appealing setting I can imagine: a sandy beach, a hammock in the yard, the slope of a grassy hill. I project absolute stillness in that setting and the warmth of the sun washing over me. Then I let go. With body and mind fully relaxed, I become a crystal-clear vessel — ready to receive and use spiritual communication. I've learned to meditate as the need arises. This simple technique can help me to relax in the middle of confusion; it can also help me to prepare for an important meeting or presentation, then restore me afterwards.

Meditation is a helpful tool when I get nervous or very excited. That happens less frequently now, but it *does* happen. I still get uptight when I'm stuck in traffic or running late for an appointment. One reason this doesn't happen as much anymore is that I plan better and leave a lot earlier for appointments. That's one way not to get anxious about traffic or time. If I'm going to be late, though, and there's nothing I can do about it, I just tell myself to relax and be calm. I take a deep breath and ask myself the worst thing that could happen. I might be reprimanded or embarrassed; I might lose my client or some money. I acknowledge the fear and reality of what might happen. I just relax and I don't try to avoid that reality. What can I do about it? Not a thing. But I *can* be calm. I've learned to meditate in seconds almost any place I go. Of course, this has taken lots of practice and experience. It's been worth it, though. Having the ability to get out of my body and open up my mind to think and hear clearly is a real blessing.

The Big Book says that we will know instinctively when we are in conscious communication with God, rather than hearing ourselves, as I did at first. Believe me, when it happened I knew and the feeling I had made me eager to repeat the experience. I discovered that meditation was a good way for me to work through my skepticism about a Higher Power. I began having long conversations with my Higher Power and learned to work out my problems while in conscious communication with Him. Now my life is made richer each day through dialogues with my God.

I pray to God for the knowledge and power to carry out His will. This means, for example, even if I don't have abstinence tomorrow, I want to get through today. I really don't know *anyone* who has *perfect* abstinence from compulsive overeating. When I acknowledge that I've eaten compulsively I say, "God, if that's Your will for me, fine. I don't want to do this anymore. So I ask Your will for me and the power to carry it out. If that means that I will gain weight again, I come without reservation." Now, this is hard to do, especially when old habits make me want to take matters into my own hands and say, "God, I want you to do this or prevent that." Many people, I think carry around a reward/punishment notion about God. They believe that God will give them what they want if they're good but that He'll block their wishes and dreams if they're bad. I grew up with the idea that a person goes either to heaven or hell. But I always bargained with myself by saying, "Well, I can mess things up today because I've got other days to make it up and swing the score to my advantage." I figured that if the scale was even slightly tipped toward the good, God would notice and assure me a place in heaven. Times when I felt destined to go to hell, I'd say, "Well, I don't believe in that whole heaven and hell idea anyway." Rationalizations like this followed me into adulthood and kept me out of hell, or so I thought. When I came to the Program, I realized I'd been in hell all along and that heaven was within my reach anytime I really wanted it.

I approach the Program unconditionally now in asking God's will and the power to carry it out. That is all I have the right to ask for. I can't dictate to God, can't ask Him to right wrongs or perform tasks in my life. At times, I still find it difficult to ask for God's will and not get what I thought I wanted. This is when the power I've prayed for — power to carry out God's will becomes so important. I've prayed for the power to accept God's will and work with it, knowing that in the end, it will benefit my life. Things don't always work out as I wish they would, but the bottom line is that I want to feel good *in spite* of that fact. The power I receive from God can help me to maintain calmness and serenity in the face of potentially upsetting circumstances.

An example from my own life illustrated this power in use. I come from a family background of yelling and screaming. To this day, when somebody yells, I automatically tense up, feel guilty. For a moment, I'm in a state of anxiety that is terrifically uncomfortable, even if I'm not directly involved. By using my God-given power though, I can carry whatever serenity and good feelings I have right through that situation and emerge without the anxiety and guilt. At the very least, I can reduce my anxiety response to that of a split second.

The Program has given me the ability to work through a problem and, when that effort isn't satisfactory, it's given me resilience to bounce back quickly. The Program is now my fortification and support — something I can turn to that will restore and refresh me. It beats any kind of food I've ever tasted. This Program has literally bought me that critical split second that exists between sanity and insanity:

- I'm just about to eat something compulsively. Now I get a split second before I put the food in my mouth, a split second that allows me to make a choice. I know I don't have to eat this food to survive . . . so I don't eat it.
- I'm just about to jump out of my car and curse someone out for his driving habits. Now I get a split second before I jump out and let loose with the language, a split second that allows me to make a choice. I know I don't have to curse at that person in order to get my point across . . . so I don't.

It's a great freedom, being relieved of my compulsions. I no longer waste precious time and energy on former obsessions — getting even, taking revenge, eating. Instead, I get split seconds when I need them now, reprieves from insanity when I can reaffirm myself and my responsibility. In so doing, I make my choices. Those seconds are a gift from God that make me a happier, healthier person each day of my life.

High states of anxiety used to completely paralyze me. That still happens, but much less frequently now. Anxiety is no longer so apt to control me. In the past, an anxiety attack would have left me feeling terrible and weak. Automatically, I would have fortified myself with food. Now, I just take a little time with those feelings and gradually work myself out of them. Calmness and serenity return without the guilt or the panic or the food. Some people eat to numb psychic pain. I did that, but I also ate when I felt good. This made for almost constant eating. When I felt depressed or angry or frightened, I ate to both justify and perpetuate the feeling. At times when things were going well and I still felt bad, I'd eat to explain that incongruity and to produce a little guilt to keep it going. So my advice is to fight those reactions; don't play those games with food and feelings. Do anything you can think of to avoid eating at those critical times: pray, meditate, go for a walk, call a friend. If you do break down and eat, though, don't be too hard on yourself for it. Acknowledge that you've weakened, then resolve to make a fresh start the next day. You might begin by calling a friend and telling that person about the Program. When people call me and lament that they've binged, I say, "So what?"

"So what?! It's horrible!" they'll answer back.

But I just say, "Yeah, it's horrible, but that was yesterday. How long are you going to hang on to that?"

The Big Book says, "In the promise we will be relieved." For overeaters, this means we will be relieved of our insanity about food. Now this doesn't guarantee that we're going to be *thin*. In fact, nowhere in the Big Book does it guarantee anything but freedom from compulsions. Instead, it says we will be relieved of the necessity of having to drink (eat) compulsively.

The woman who introduced me to this Program used to be my secretary. Not long ago, she worked for me again during my regular secretary's vacation. After her first day back she said to me, "You've changed; you're a nicer person." I thought that was the best compliment possible from someone who knew me years ago. She saw a definite change in my reaction to work crises, too. I no longer get upset or excited about such things. I don't know why I'm not uptight in those situations anymore, but I'm not. I can't really explain how or why the depression I felt has given way to happiness. But I know one thing for sure: the more I read the Twelve Steps and work the Program, the happier I feel.

Step Twelve

"Having had a spiritual awakening as the result of these steps, we tried to carry this message to other compulsive overeaters, and to practice these principles in all our affairs."

"To practice these principles," as the Twelfth Step says, is the key to the payoff of the Program for us. The more we give of ourselves, the more our self-esteem goes up and our weight goes down. In other words, our self-image grows and our weight diminishes in direct proportion to the growth of our ability to give of ourselves in true humility. This is the true meaning of our Twelfth Step, our Program, and of happiness achieved through God.

When I first read the Twelfth Step, this is how it sounded to me: "Having had this spiritual experience, we tell other fat people how to do what we want them to do and this is really what the Program is about." The Twelfth Step seemed to me like an open invitation to once again play God. Strange, how in our desire to play God we hear what we want to hear, read what we want to read, and practice whatever will give us power.

Most people come to the Program fat and full of self-will. I was no different. In fact, I floundered around for a long time, actually *thinking* I was working the Program. All I was really doing was dieting, memorizing some words and spouting my version of the Program to anyone who cared to listen. Not enough. What I needed was inspiration, something to move me on toward that spiritual awakening the Twelfth Step talks about.

The first eleven steps are training steps, a preparation for our new reality. By consistently working these steps in all areas of our lives, we become spiritually attuned to God. The process reminds me a little of marathon running. If I want to be classified as a marathoner I must, by definition, be able to run twenty-six miles. There is no shortcut to this distinction; training is absolutely fundamental to running that distance. Without the training, I would be unable to run the distance — no matter *what* I called myself. The first eleven steps train us to become what we are ultimately meant to be — mature, open, and loving people in touch with God and His will for us.

Anyone can diet, but we really need to learn how to maintain. This Program is essentially one of maintenance. When I greet newcomers I say, "We're here to help you maintain a level of spirituality and a state of mind, and the end result will be that you'll never get fat again. Isn't that a lot better than dieting?" I tell them, "Just stick around and see what you can find. I didn't understand the Program at first and we don't expect that you will, either."

As compulsive overeaters, we have really created our own problems; food is only a symbol and fat a symptom. We have a serious problem with food that affects us every day of our lives. The compulsion has come to permeate every aspect of our lives and it's capable of destroying us. Now, if I'm destined to be a compulsive eater for the rest of my life, then I might as well act that out by eating. If I have to go through the tortures of hell each day to resist the temptations of food, then I might as well eat. I'm going to die anyway, I might as well anesthetize myself with food.

But when we come to acknowledge our compulsiveness and really accept ourselves as we are, as the Big Book says, we are given some hope. It says that we can and will recover. We can overcome the act of compulsive overeating but, more important, we can also overcome the *desire* to eat compulsively. Our lives don't need to be a struggle.

I've heard lots of people in AA make a careful distinction between sobriety and working the Program. They say that abstinence alone is nothing. I really don't agree. I maintain that abstinence is better than the old compulsive behaviors. Dieting is better than overeating; not drinking is better than being drunk. It's true, though, that abstinence represents only a small improvement. The spiritual malady persists unless you're working the Program. It's unfortunate, I think, when people lose weight without working the Program. We need and deserve so much *more!* I wanted a lot more than just a weight loss — I wanted happiness, good health and freedom from worry about foods and diets. What I wanted was recovery.

I can tell you this: a spiritual experience was absolutely essential for my recovery. I can also tell you that the experience didn't come fast and it didn't come easily. As I meet other people joining the Program, I always hope that their spiritual awakening will come faster than mine did. But then, each of us is different, and we come to terms with spirituality in our own time. In Dr. Bob's story in the Big Book, he tells how he had his first real spiritual experience after two and a half years of sobriety. If it took Dr. Bob that long, I think we can be patient and allow ourselves some time.

I did everything backwards for such a long time. I'd plan my priorities like this: "First, I'll lose weight; second, I'll straighten my head out; and finally, if I have the time and patience, I'll try to get a little religion." Time after time, I'd try to redirect my life this way. But I'd always fail; eventually my plan would give way and I'd be back with my old behavior. The Big Book is quite clear when it says that only *after* the spiritual malady is taken care of will other things be corrected. All those years, it was pointless for me to work on the physical and mental aspects of my life without first working on my spirituality. This Program can free us from those temporary, self-defeating plans to improve our lives.

I always assumed a spiritual experience would be a real drama: I'd instantly be charged with a great dynamic force. Of course, it didn't work out that way. Even when I actually had that first spiritual experience, my expectations about it were still unrealistic. I was surprised, having undergone this "transformation," that I still had to wait an hour and fifteen minutes at the airport for my luggage. I thought that somebody who'd had a spiritual experience would surely get his luggage back right away. (Shows how much the airline people thought about my spiritual experience!) A later spiritual experience told me it was okay to wait for my baggage. Since that time, I have learned to actually *enjoy* an unexpected wait for my luggage. It gives me a chance to look around at other people and their reactions; it also gives me time to think.

A welling-up inside or a feeling of well-being that fills your consciousness — that's really the best way I can describe my own spiritual experiences. The Big Book describes it in terms of feeling "safe and protected." When you're in fit spiritual condition, you just feel comfortable and sure that God is with you at all times.

For me, getting to that point could only be accomplished by living each of the Twelve Steps. The longer I live those steps, the more I feel comfortable and sure about myself and others and have no desire to eat compulsively. I've come to like myself even though I'm not always doing good things. What counts for me is that I'm doing more good things than I've ever done before. I'm a nice person, probably not terrific, but I never get down on myself anymore. I don't have that bottom line feeling that I'm basically bad.

I've come to terms with my fantasies. I know that I'll never achieve some of the goals I've had for my life. I was going to be governor of California someday. It never worked out, never will. But I can accept that and move ahead to concentrate on goals that *are* attainable. I do have something now that I never thought possible, and that is peace of mind. I'd venture a guess that most people who come into the Program think that thinness will bring them happiness. That's not the way it works. Instead, real happiness and self-acceptance make it unnecessary, even unthinkable, to abuse alcohol, drugs, or food. The greatest spiritual experience of all lies within you.

Traditionally, well-meaning people have told alcoholics, overeaters, and drug-abusers that their obsession will disappear if they just forget about their own selfish interests and serve others. The founders of AA recognized that this advice just wasn't getting results. Just helping others wasn't enough. They knew they had to devise a way to motivate people to help *themselves* by helping others.

I came to the Program with little or no interest in helping others. Like most compulsive people, I was completely absorbed in my own problems and needs. Careful and continuous practice of the first eleven steps was my agent of change. Gradually, I became a different person with new values and priorities. My interest in others was now genuine, an outgrowth of the real pleasure I came to feel in serving as an instrument of God without any thought of reward. There are several Biblical stories that portray true charity as the act of giving anonymously. This is the kind of giving that is really most rewarding. It's a joyous secret between you and your God.

The Big Book says that helping others is essential to our recovery. But the attitude of reaching out and helping isn't something we just slip into at meetings or when we encounter a member of the Program. We must be willing, every day and in all aspects of our lives, to be Good Samaritans.

Being that Good Samaritan is no easy task. According to the Big Book, "It may mean the loss of many nights' sleep, great interference with your pleasures, interruptions to your business." It goes on to say that being the Good Samaritan "may mean sharing your money and your home, counselling frantic wives and relatives, innumerable trips to police courts, sanitariums, hospitals, jails . . . "(p. 97).

One Sunday morning, I was enthusiastically looking forward to a game of tennis. I'd just returned from an OA retreat in Oregon and hadn't played for three weeks. It was a beautiful morning, so I headed for the tennis club, and we started playing about 10:30. Minutes into our first game, I was notified there was a call for me. Frustrated by the interruption, I went into the clubhouse and took the phone.

"Bill, you don't know me," the caller said, "but I go to your Monday meetings and I've heard you talk about this Twelve Step work. I want to tell you that I have a friend who just overdosed. Would you be willing to go over to the hospital and see him?"

I said, "Are you kidding? I just came back from doing four days of OA work. This is my first chance to relax in weeks, and I'm in the middle of a tennis game."

"But you said that helping others can save *your* life," she said.

I told her that I'd saved my life a lot that week and that her request could wait a day or so. She gave me the name of her friend and said she'd call back.

I hung up and went back to my tennis game with the conversation nagging at me. Finally at noon I said, "Darn it. Forget the tennis game." I showered, drove to the hospital, and checked on this man. He was barely conscious and he was alone. His family lived in another part of the country, and his friends were reluctant to visit him, fearing inquiries about drug use. Looking at him, all I could think of was how I'd feel in that situation. I pinned a note with my name and phone number to his hospital gown.

He said very little but that wasn't the point. You *see*, I knew that I needed this man more than he needed me because that's the length I will go to to save my life. At that moment, I was in fit spiritual condition, as close to God as I ever get.

That is what keeping spiritually fit is all about — being your brother's keeper, doing for others, really *living* that Golden Rule. If you did nothing but go out and do these things, God would remove your insanity. But we have nothing to give to others until our own lives are in order. Working the Twelve Steps and staying close to God will prepare us for reaching out effectively. Frankly, I don't know any other way to help people except through the Twelve Steps. I don't carry around any exclusive knowledge or magic formula. What I do have is a willingness to share my own experiences with the steps, and how they work for me. If sharing those experiences can help others, that's great. Of course, the ultimate answer is always to let go of the problem and let God take care of it.

It says in the Big Book on page 90, "When you discover a prospect for Alcoholic's Anonymous, find out all you can about him . . . Get an idea of his behavior, his problems, his background . . . You need this information to put yourself in his place, to see how you would like him to approach you if the tables were turned. Sometimes it is wise to wait till he goes on a binge." If he does not want to stop drinking, don't waste time trying to persuade him.

Those ideas translate well to our work with compulsive overeaters. Too often, I think, we feel *so* responsible, like the Lone Ranger coming to save people from themselves. We've got enough to do to manage just rescuing ourselves! We don't need to worry about rescuing others. We're not out to rescue anybody; we're out to share what we have. If people don't want what we have, there's not much we can do about it, but we *can* keep trying. The Big Book says we should continue to talk about alcoholism (translate that to compulsive overeating) as "an illness, a fatal malady. Talk about conditions of body and mind which accompany it. Keep his attention focused mainly on your personal experience."

I'm so thankful that someone talked to me at that first meeting I attended and said, "If you have a better place to go, go there." When that comment forced me to consider my options, I realized that I had none. I'd tried everything and had nowhere else to go. In a last-ditch effort to save my life, I decided to stick around for a while and give the Program a chance. Everything was a puzzle to me at first. To complicate things, I felt resentful when people talked about God. Writing those people off in my mind as religious fanatics, I just didn't want to *hear* what they had to say. I did sense, however, that these people were being honest with me.

Any newcomer is a challenge to those already working the Program. Shortcuts don't help people; we have to wait until they're really ready for help. Sometimes they'll keep right on bingeing. Let them. I just don't think the Program helps people until they're hurting, until they have nowhere else to turn.

Not long ago, I met a medical doctor who told me about a woman he had interviewed for an insurance exam. When it came out that she had recently lost seventy pounds, he asked her how she had accomplished that. She told him that she'd joined an organization free of charge, lost the weight, and kept it off. Simple enough. She went on to explain the Program with the doctor only half-listening. Then, about six months later, the doctor's weight was literally killing him. Vaguely remembering the mention of an organization that helped a patient lose weight, he spent hours searching his files. He finally found the name and started attending meetings. When I met him six months later, he'd lost ninety pounds. Now that patient who told him about the Program might have thought that what she said to him went in one ear and out the other. But people *do hear* . And when they're ready to connect with our message, they will.

When people I sponsor feel they're having a problem with food again, they know exactly what my recommendation is to them: *don't call me, call someone else and see if you can help them.* Working with others must become part of our lifestyle. On page 102 the Big Book says, "Your job now is to be at the place where you may be of maximum helpfulness to others, so never hesitate to go anywhere if you can be helpful. You should not hesitate to visit the most sordid spot on earth on such an errand. Keep on the firing line of life with these motives and God will keep you unharmed." If you have anger, go find an angry person. If you feel selfish, go find a selfish person. If you can't find an angry person or a selfish person, find a compulsive overeater, an alcoholic or a drug addict and ask, "What can I do for you?"

Many people think they'll be terribly embarrassed to go out and find others. But think about it for a minute — why on earth should we be embarrassed to share a program that works for us? Remember, we're not forcing ourselves or our ideas on anyone, we're making ourselves accessible to others if and when they need us. This is not to say that we don't take risks. To live fully, we must take risks all the time.

Think about friendship — a real friend is someone who is willing to put the friendship on the line and be honest. A friend will say to you that you've put on some weight and it's an observation, not a judgment. Personally, I want to surround myself with people who are willing to risk everything to be straight and honest with me. The person who hedges about being honest and says, "Gee, I don't want to hurt your feelings," isn't really a friend. He's a person who's afraid to hurt my feelings because maybe then I won't like him. I want people around me who are choosing to be there rather than needing to be there.

I know a man in the Program who had lost one hundred and forty pounds but still had another fifty to lose in order to reach his goal. Instead of continuing to lose, though, he started to gain weight again. No one really wanted to approach this man about his weight gain; they didn't want to be in the position of taking his inventory for him. Finally one day, I asked him to lunch and took the risk of asking about his progress.

Straight out I said to him. "When are you going to lose the rest of that weight?"

Instead of being angry, he acknowledged his problem right away, concluding that he needed "a stricter diet."

"Are you willing to accept the fact that maybe that's all the weight you're going to lose?" I asked and waited for his reaction. Well, that was just a horrible thought to him because he wanted perfection. I said to him, "Maybe this weight is what God has in mind for you now. If you're working a good Program, the weight will come off. If this is all that is to come off, then accept that for now. Until you're willing to let go and accept yourself as you are, nothing more is going to happen."

I need to feel really confident within myself to be so straightforward with other people. But, that is what's needed. We must consistently look to the basics — the Twelve Steps of recovery. We can deal with any of our compulsions or insanities through these steps.

The Big Book says that one cannot be *cured* of alcoholism, (even though Bill W. did use the word in his story). That probably holds true with compulsive overeating too. I think what we have is a daily reprieve from our compulsions, contingent on our spiritual condition. Resentment, jealousy, envy, frustration, and fear — powerful enemies of the compulsive overeater — are the feelings most likely to pull us back to old patterns of eating. But we cannot afford to have those feelings anymore or the behavior that goes with them. To stay in fit spiritual condition is to keep those negative feelings from entering and dominating our lives.

We must always remember that our recovery is grounded in our dependence upon God, not our dependence upon other people. If we really trust in Him and the power He gives us, we can recover and never again worry about problems with food. Think for a minute about the freedom of never again having to say, "I can't eat that . . . " Instead, with trust in God, we will be able to honestly say to ourselves, "I *choose* not to eat that because I have no desire to eat it." There is a world of difference between dieting and having God remove the desire for food, allowing us to react normally and sanely. We can bring new quality to our lives and make healthy choices about food, so long as we stay in fit spiritual condition. Furthermore, a life without food compulsion has new meaning. Our days will be measured not by meal times but by experiences; moments in time will be shaped not by what we've had to eat but by our relationship with God and the help we've given to others.

By working on our relationship with God and our attitude of helping others, we can establish a strong and positive base for living happily with ourselves and with the other people in our lives — our friends, our family, our co-workers, the guy in the car behind us, the neighbor moving in down the street. We need not be victims of our environment; we can let go and let God work His miracle in our lives.

Why Diets Will Not Work

Sharing is giving of yourself and getting back from others their willingness to receive that gift. A lot of people, especially those who are new to the Program, find hope in knowing that others have been where they are now.

This book is my sharing.

The only way I ever learn is through pain and suffering. When others in the Program first told me that, I thought it was a horrible thing to say to anybody. I wanted to learn and grow through joy and pleasure! But unfortunately there is always pain in growing. Only when I hurt am I willing to move and take a step forward. I am willing to change only when the pain of where I am is worse than the anticipated pain of where I'm going.

We all hope that we will lose weight and keep it off. The miracle for me was that, after taking off seventy-five pounds, I kept those pounds off for three and a half years working the kind of Program that is not really a Program at all, but just a lot of good diets.

I accomplished this through sheer ego and fear — fear of losing my new friends in the Program, because I was sure I'd be a disappointment to them and that they would no longer like me if I put the weight back on. I was afraid of losing the respect they seemed to have for me because of my weight loss, which was a unique achievement at the time I came into the Program. Now there are many more success stories.

Through the years I have noticed that those who come into the Program and don't believe they are know-it-alls seem to be able to catch on faster.

One day I met a fellow who weighed about four hundred pounds. He was jaded and callous and could intellectualize the shirt off your back. Someone planned a meeting for us in a restaurant. I had never seen him before, but as soon as I walked in, I knew who he was — a four-hundred-pound chain smoker with drinks lined up in front of him. The minute I sat down he said, "Let's eat."

He knew why I was there, but at the time he would not even admit that he was fat.

We talked. I just shared what I had. I said that I had been very fat at one time and I worked this Program. He had heard of Alcoholics Anonymous, so I explained that this was similar. Then I said, "Why don't you come to a meeting? If you'd like to come, here's my telephone number. Call me. If you don't want to come, that's perfectly okay, too. We can still be friends. But you'd be doing me a favor if you came."

He did come to a meeting. He sat in the back of the room "doing research" and did not take part. Afterwards, he came up to me and asked, "Where's this diet sheet?"

"We ran out of them," I said, "but come back next week."

The next week when he returned, he said, "Where is that gray-sheet diet they talk about?"

I said the literature chairman had not received them, but why didn't he come back the following week? The third week when he appeared and the gray sheets still had not arrived, he was a little upset. He let me know in no uncertain terms that he was there to get the diet.

I said, "I can't understand what happened. We just don't seem to have any."

As he shares it now, he sat in the back and, as he looked around at the couple of hundred others in the room, he began to wonder why they were there. If they weren't getting a diet, what were they listening to? So he began to listen, too.

Now he has lost one hundred and forty-five pounds. He married a wonderful woman in the Program, who has also lost over one hundred pounds. He is an incredible person. But he never found the diet.

That is how I practice the Program. I don't diet, and I don't sponsor people who diet. I don't even talk to people about food except to say, "That's very interesting." Instead, I say, "How are things going today? What steps are you working? How about reading chapter so-and-so in the Big Book? It might help solve your problem."

One woman who was having a lot of trouble with food asked if I would be willing to talk to her on the telephone each morning and discuss her diet. I said, "No, but I'll be very happy if you will call me up every morning and we can discuss the first three steps. Let's find out if that will work."

We compulsive overeaters have a threefold illness — physical, emotional, and spiritual — but all too often we have only a onefold program: the physical part. The Twelve Step Program is first, last, and always a spiritual program.

I believe that the purpose of this Program is to guide us to a spiritual contact with God, as we understand Him. When that happens, not only will we lose weight, but our desire for food will be taken away. The compulsion will be removed.

Mahatma Gandhi, one of the world's great spiritual leaders, said: "I know that it is argued that the soul has nothing to do with what one eats or drinks, as a soul neither eats nor drinks — that it is not what you put inside you from without but what you express outwardly from within that matters. There is no doubt, but rather than examine this reasoning, I shall content myself with merely declaring my firm conviction that for the seeker who would live in fear of God and who would see Him face to face, restraint in diet, both as to quantity and quality, is as essential as restraint . . . restraint as in thought and speech."

Many of us who come to this Program want only to diet and lose weight. But losing weight does not solve the problem of compulsive overeating.

All my life, I tried to lose weight, and I have lost, successfully, on every diet I undertook. But I always put the pounds back on. This time I have lost weight and kept it off. Why? Because God is doing it. I have given up dieting. I no longer care what, where, or when I eat, because food does not hold a priority in my life. The Big Book says it on page 84, "God is doing for us what we could not do for ourselves."

My "diet" is to get "thin" in the head, and the body will follow. I have never seen it fail — those who work the spiritual Program lose weight and keep it off.

To those who want diets or rules and regulations: Remember that we are looking for results, not methods; for sanity, not telling other people how to live; for recovery, not dwelling in the disease. We are looking for freedom from food compulsions, rather than being tied up in the problem. ("Woe is me! I'm a compulsive overeater with this horrible disease.")

I used to feel deprived when I dieted. And when we compulsive overeaters are denied something, we begin to build up resentments. But we get even! I always got even by putting on weight . . . that really showed you, didn't it?!

There is an enormous difference between having no appetite for chocolate cake — and therefore not eating it — and not eating chocolate cake because it makes me fat. I was told when I came into the Program that I had this terrible illness called compulsive overeating which I would always have, that I would be fighting my tendency to overeat all my life. At that time, I never heard anyone say that the compulsion could be removed.

As a child I was programmed to feel that I was bad. When I grew up, I sought to prove that those people who thought I was bad were all wrong. But a little message in the back of my head kept repeating the old programming, so I felt, "They were really right, weren't they?"

Nevertheless I was going to do things my way, which had always led me — and those around me — down the path to destruction. I bulldozed myself into many terrible situations in life, and I became an expert at rationalization. For instance, I used to think I wasn't fat, I was just short for my weight!

The purpose of the Program is not to teach you how to lose weight. If you are looking for an easier, softer, more definitive way to be inspired to diet, you are not going to find it in a Twelve Step Program. I have no magic words of inspiration to make you want to diet. I don't know how anybody can diet any differently than to stop eating whatever it is that produces fat. It has taken me a long time to grasp the differences between dieting and the Program.

Every time I think I understand the Program completely, it unfolds a little more for me. Now I believe I have the concept of it, and it's based on a very simple premise: *all of us compulsive overeaters, one way or another, have been programmed to feel bad about ourselves.*

Sometimes a person will protest, "But I have had great parents and a wonderful childhood." Still, for all of us, whether we are compulsive overeaters or alcoholics or other drug addicts, we have thought somewhere along the line that we are inadequate or somehow "no good." Unless we can accept that premise, the concept of the Program is going to be very difficult.

No matter what we compulsive types do, we still feel bad about ourselves. Quite simply, we don't like ourselves. We can get the greatest jobs in the world, find the perfect lovers, have the most loving families, yet we still don't feel good about ourselves! That's because we have been programmed intentionally or unintentionally, through parents, peers, or otherwise — to feel that we are not worthwhile.

One of the obvious ways people begin to feel bad about themselves is by feeling ugly, especially in a society which places such emphasis on beauty. In a culture where pierced ear lobes which hang down in big circles are considered beautiful, you would feel ugly walking around with your regular, non-drooping ear lobes.

When we look back to see what was thought to be attractive in the days of the silent movies, we find that women actresses were at least ten pounds overweight by today's standards. If you look at pictures of people in our society in the 1880s, you'll see that women with big bosoms and big behinds or men with big bellies were acceptable.

Nowadays, it is definitely in style to be thin. If we are not thin, we begin to feel left out, which fortifies our feeling of being not okay. In our society, fat people are not okay.

How do we get to be fat? We overeat or we eat the wrong things. Some of us have used excuses: "I'm big-boned" or "I have this underactive thyroid" or "My metabolism is messed up." While excuses serve no purpose, each one of us has a unique problem with food. For some of us, flour and refined sugar seem to trigger weight gain. But I also know those who *can* eat flour and sugar; these are not their binge foods. I won't go into the consequences of eating certain foods; let's leave that to the food chemists and nutritionists.

We just need to accept that: 1) we feel bad about ourselves, and the way we continue to feel bad is by being fat; 2) we're fat because we overeat.

Our assumption is that we feel bad *because* we are fat, that if we get thin, then of course we'll feel good. This may work for a while, but how do we stop overeating forever?

Here's the problem: I have fifty pounds to lose, and I'm going to start on a diet. It takes a long time to lose fifty pounds, and along the way — since I am programmed to feel bad about myself — I am not going to feel terrific. The only time I will feel really great, supposedly, is when I lose all fifty of those pounds.

However, since I am programmed to feel bad, I still won't feel good about myself, even when I lose the weight. So, I eventually will put it back on. You see, having lost it, there is no way to explain why I feel bad except that I feel guilty about putting it back on. So I binge and get to feeling *really* bad again.

This is what I have learned on the Program and what I would like to share: we compulsive overeaters all feel bad about ourselves. And we make sure we continue to feel bad about ourselves by being fat, by overeating.

We believe that the way to feel good is to eat less, go on a diet or a food plan, and lose weight. This does not work. Some of us have lost a considerable amount of weight, only to put it on again. Or, even if we have not regained the pounds, we still — surprisingly — don't feel good about ourselves. *The problem is that we are not feeling bad because we are fat; we use being fat as an excuse!*

We make up other excuses, too, as reasons to feel bad. I have a rotten marriage. My parents didn't love me. My kids are ungrateful. My job is dull. The weather is too hot, or too cold. We can point to hundreds of reasons why we feel bad. They all seem logical. They are not.

Why do we use these excuses, especially the excuse of being fat? Well, food, first of all, is special to each of us. Somewhere, sometime, we ate the first meal that started us on the path to being compulsive overeaters. You could just as easily have had the first drink and turned into an alcoholic or started a first fire and been an arsonist. There are a multitude of compulsions! Why ours is food instead of something else is not important.

Also, we use fat as an excuse for feeling bad because if we didn't have an excuse for being depressed and upset, we might end up in mental institutions. Imagine that the thermometer reads one hundred degrees in the shade and I report that I feel cold. There is nothing wrong with my reporting that I feel cold when I can explain that I have a health problem. However, if I act out my feeling cold when it's one hundred degrees outside by walking around the streets in a fur coat complaining that I'm freezing, I probably am going to be locked up! So I have to say that I have a health problem which seems to affect my body temperature. That's understandable, so no one thinks I'm insane.

In the same way, when I say I feel ugly and terrible and have no sense of self-worth because I'm fat, that is logical and credible. You see, if we were thin and rich and had marvelous husbands and wives and great jobs, and still felt terrible, then we would seem to need psychiatric help. But as long as we throw out excuses, we seem perfectly sane. Putting it in very simple terms, the real reason we eat compulsively is to keep from getting locked up — so people will think we're sane. If we weren't fat, we would have no apparent reason for feeling bad.

We don't make up these excuses consciously, of course. It is instinctive. As little children, we learned that if we ran away from someone who was trying to hit us, we were not going to get hurt. If a bully comes at us with a club, we don't stop to think, "Oh, a person with a club. Perhaps I am going to get hurt. The thing to do now is run." We take to our heels instinctively.

Instinctively, too, we find excuses for feeling bad about ourselves — dozens of them. Compulsive overeaters as children were programmed to use food. *We eat in order to be fat in order to explain our low self-images.* The irony is that all our lives we have told ourselves that we want to feel good, to be happy, and that we can accomplish this by eating less and getting thin. Of course, dieting or following a food plan works for a while, but as a permanent way of feeling good, it won't. I don't know anyone who has gained a sense of personal value simply by losing weight and ending the change there.

Some people will tell you that we have to get started on our weight loss first, so that we can start feeling *a little bit* good about ourselves. Then we can go on to work the Program. But there is nothing worse than getting rid of the reason you think you feel bad and still feeling bad! How many of us who have lost all of our extra weight can remember reaching our goal and saying, "Is this it? I've achieved my weight loss, and I don't seem to feel any better or any worse than before."

We have to acknowledge that we sometimes do things backwards. If we can learn to feel good about ourselves, then the reason for being fat ceases. If we don't have to be fat anymore because we feel good, then we will stop our compulsive overeating automatically.

As we lose the need to be fat, we lose the need to overeat. Thus, the Program promises that we will lose our appetites automatically. So what the Program has meant to me is this: if I could feel good about myself, I would stop the compulsive activities which I had needed to make me feel bad. *There is no sense in being fat in order to continue to feel bad when I don't feel bad anymore.*

Even though people may talk about me or put me down, I still like me. If I like me all the time, if I have peace of mind, if I can say, "I messed up my life today, but I'm okay anyhow," then I will never have to diet.

It is impossible for a compulsive overeater who has developed a feeling of self-worth to continue to eat compulsively.

Don't misinterpret me and say, "I heard Bill tell us that if we work the Program, we can eat anything." That's not it at all. I, for one, know that flour and sugar make me fat. As a practicing compulsive overeater, I'm going to eat flour and sugar. I am also going to eat celery stalks and broccoli and the tablecloth and whatever else is not nailed down. I am crazy when it comes to food. However, when I feel good about myself, being fat is incompatible with my image of myself. I don't have to be fat anymore to explain my bad feelings. Therefore I lose my appetite. When food is around, I react "sanely and normally," as the Big Book promises (p. 85).

I know if I have a piece of bread, I am not going to put on twenty pounds. That piece of bread will not create an overwhelming craving in me which would make me want to eat an entire loaf. If I had a piece of bread, however, then I must figure how to cut down on the next meal. Why bother with all that figuring? I just don't eat bread in the first place. We don't have to diet anymore if we really lose our appetites.

How do we begin to build that important sense of self-worth? Through the spiritual experience that, for me at least, comes only by living the Twelve Step Program.

The Program works not on how to eat or how to control what we take in. It does not aim to brainwash us or teach discipline or behavior modification. It simply gives us the opportunity to become a totally different person — a spiritual person. The Big Book talks about a change in our state of mind, in which new attitudes, motives, and desires begin to dominate our lives. Emotionally, we change completely.

The term "spiritual" has frightened some people away from the Twelve Step Program. But as many as have been scared away have stayed around and tried to understand its meaning.

I used to laugh at spirituality. I had no interest in it and I thought anyone who did was crazy. But now I know this: God exists for me because I allow it.

No diets or shock therapies or mental disciplines are ever going to have the effect upon us that the spiritual experience of these Twelve Steps will. Anyone can have spirituality through the process of these steps. That's why we continue to live them until they become a way of life.

Also, you can always learn something more about the Program. One of these days suddenly the principles will hit home, and you will say, "So, *that's* what this Program is all about!" Finally you will understand that the spiritual experience that comes through the Twelve Steps makes us like ourselves better.

Food has nothing to do with being fat. Food is just a vehicle we use to keep on not liking ourselves. Worrying about food is like zeroing in on the spark plugs when the problem is the entire automobile.

Overeating is not really the problem; it is the symptom. I am no more the effect of what I weigh, any more than I am the effect of how old I am, what kinds of relationships I have, or how much money I earn. Although it is nice to be thin, financially secure, and happy in relationships, what we believe to be the causes of happiness are not necessarily valid for us. Some of us have been rich and then poor, married and then divorced. But if we really look at our lives, these things have not made much difference in how happy we feel. We have been lonely when we were single and sometimes lonelier when we were married.

There isn't one of us who hasn't come into this Program thinking that happiness would be automatic if we were only thin. The truth is that when a person is happy within herself or himself, then there is no necessity to drink too much, eat too much, drive a car too fast, or lie about income taxes.

That, to me, is the message of this Program.

The problem is emotional, the symptom is physical, the solution is spiritual. So why diet?

Abstinence

In talking about my definition of abstinence, I want to be very clear up front that I don't speak for anyone but myself. What I say here is based on strictly my feelings, my experience, my interpretation of my Program. I know it works for me.

Abstinence is a term that is difficult to explain. When someone says, "I am on abstinence," that person is following a prescribed and controlled method of eating, usually designed to lose weight, but not necessarily so.

When we come into Overeaters Anonymous, we are told that it is not a diet club. A piece of paper is handed to each of us which, by its own admission, is not a diet, but a food plan. But I believe that the definition of a diet *is* a controlled method of eating. A food plan *is* a controlled method of eating and, therefore, a diet.

The next thing we are told is that we should get a "food sponsor." The first function of a food sponsor is to advise you about what to eat; but all too often, another function of a food sponsor is to manipulate and control your life.

There is a difference between the food plan kind of "abstinence," and what the Program sets forth as real abstinence. For some people, abstinence means simply a controlled, revised, forced and pressured way of eating. Of the two interpretations of abstinence — this pressure and control method is an easier, softer way. But like all easier, softer ways, it must be kept up forever; otherwise we fail. If we interpret abstinence this way, we must discipline ourselves to weigh and measure our foods and to call in our food to a sponsor forever. This way will work and does for many.

Having a food sponsor and following a food plan can create a lot of pressure and guilt. The effect of this pressure is to emphasize deprivation of food — something we compulsive overeaters have felt all our lives. The question is whether we want to continue to lose weight through guilt, pressure, and deprivation. Or is there another way? The answer is clearly set forth in our Program — it lies in the term *abstinence,* which must be defined for each of us.

The problem is that when we come in to the Program, we admit that we are powerless — and yet we try to maintain power. The end of Chapter Five in the Big Book tells us that no human power can relieve our compulsion, but that God could and would if He were sought. Yet we persist in seeking human powers to remedy our compulsive overeating — our own willpower or self-control or the power of a food sponsor.

The Big Book says we are undisciplined. If we are undisciplined, why do we persist in seeking to discipline ourselves? So often I hear someone say, "I must have more discipline." Discipline is the last thing in the world we need or are able to have. We are powerless.

We are powerless over obtaining discipline, over controlling food, over ourselves, over other persons and situations. Why should we ever try to exercise power when it has obtained nothing for us? What we want and have always wanted is happiness, yet we have never been able to win it through our own power, manipulations, or control.

When we come in to this Program, we are unable to deal with food normally. That means that we cannot make a choice. We have no power to choose to stop eating; normal people can choose to stop eating. They can choose to eat certain things or not eat certain things. We compulsive ones have lost that power.

The Big Book tells us that we will "react sanely and normally." What that really means is that we will learn to be normal. How can we learn to be normal, to react normally? Normal people can make a decision; they have the ability to say no. Even though we have lost that ability, the ability is obtainable through God.

What we are asked to do is change our lives. We will give up all power and accept God's power. With God's power given to us through the exercise of these Twelve Steps, we will have a spiritual experience. We will "react sanely and normally." That means we will have God's power to say, "No, I don't want any more."

The difference between traditional "abstinence" and the "abstinence" promised us in the program of Overeaters Anonymous is the difference between saying, "I can't have it because it is not on my food plan" and "I choose not to have it because the compulsion is removed." There is a great difference between saying, "I can't" and "I choose not to." The difference is between exercising one's own will and discipline and calling on God's power in order to react normally and sanely.

Abstinence is not dieting; abstinence is freedom from compulsion. The Big Book tells us that this will happen automatically. If it is going to happen automatically, why are we working so hard at it? There is only one way we can stop eating compulsively, and that is if the compulsion is removed.

The definition of true abstinence is a state of being in which God has removed the compulsion from us, or at such times when it recurs we do not act on it because we have God's power to resist.

For me, the concept of God was more difficult than the concept of abstinence until somebody pointed out the words that said you don't have to *believe* in God, you just have to be willing for him to exist.

Before that, I had worked what I thought was the Program. I followed other people around who seemed to lose weight and keep it off. I emulated them, I copied them, I listened to them. I didn't just go to meetings; I went to coffee afterwards, or to their homes, or to their places of business. I would drop by and say, "Oh, I happened to be in the neighborhood." I'd talk to them or go out to lunch with them. I wanted what they had.

I didn't just want what they had at a meeting. I didn't want just the words; anyone can get up and talk. I wanted to see them at their worst, at work under pressure, or in their family settings. Whatever they had, I wanted to see it first hand. "How do I get what they have?" I kept asking, "How, how, how?"

Nobody seemed to have the wisdom I kept crying for. For years, I stayed with the Program and worked at it as best I could. My life was still filled with a compulsion for food. In fact, every day continued to be a constant struggle as I fought not to eat compulsively. Should I eat this, or should I eat that?

I was filled with righteousness because, after all, hadn't I lost weight and kept it off? And, after all, wasn't I smart and didn't I know the answers for everybody? . . . I didn't even know the answer for myself because I was still fighting my compulsion each day.

I was ready to give up. I looked at the people who came into the Program and wondered if it was really working. How many were there who had gotten thin, kept the weight off, and really had what the Program promised us? It promised that we would be relieved of our compulsion . . . and have our sanity restored. I kept asking, "Are you relieved of the compulsion?"

They would say, "No, no, we'll never be relieved of it . . . we are insane . . . we have this terrible disease."

I thought, "Is that the way it's supposed to be? If that's the way it's supposed to be, I'm not sure I want it!" I don't want to have this terrible disease — this compulsion — and I don't want to be insane. I was smart enough to know that the purpose of life was to be sane and happy, not insane and fighting each day to survive.

I thought, "I can't take it anymore. What's the use of worrying about eating this or that if I have this compulsion. Every time I drive by a doughnut shop I have a battle with myself. Every time I sit down to eat or am at a party I have a battle with myself. Sure, I didn't give in and eat compulsively, but I don't want the battle anymore! Is this the way it's supposed to be?"

In talking to alcoholics I found that some of them laughed at compulsive overeaters. (Many of them still do.) They look at us and they say, "Look at those people — all they talk about is their diets and being fat."

See, those alcoholics knew. They had been relieved of the compulsion of having to take a drink. I wanted *that*. Although I wasn't a drinker, I went to AA meetings and found something different there. They had something special.

I asked what it was and was told, "I don't know the answer either, but maybe you can find answers you are looking for in the Big Book." So I read over the Big Book of Alcoholics Anonymous, as I had many times before. And then I saw for the first time things I had never noticed.

First of all, I read the word "cured." Bill W., the founder of this Program, says, on page 191 of the Big Book, that God had *cured* him of this terrible disease. I said, "What does that mean? Others tell me I'm never going to be cured!"

Then I read a story . . . It was three in the morning . . . I just couldn't sleep because I was distressed. I got up and started looking through the Big Book and I read "We Agnostics." I had always slipped past that chapter because I wasn't an agnostic when I came into the Program, I was an atheist. I did find God, so I assumed I didn't need to read that chapter.

I read the chapter again — *really* read it this time — and at the end on page 57, it tells about an alcoholic who had been relieved of the compulsion. It says, "Save for a few brief moments of temptation, the thought of drink has never returned . . . God had restored his sanity."

I said, "Hey, I never heard those words before." Then I read again Chapter Five, "How It Works." At the very end it says that if we sought Him, God could and would relieve our compulsion. I had never really noticed those words before.

Then I read about the promise of this Program: If you work this Program, if you have a conscious contact with God, if you are in fit spiritual condition, God will remove the compulsion. This will happen not by diets or by rules. It will happen automatically.

Story after story tells us that as soon as these alcoholics had a spiritual awakening, as soon as they worked all Twelve Steps in *all* of their affairs *all* the time to the best of their ability, one day at a time, God removed their compulsions. God restored their sanity. Once again I read the Second Step of this Program: "Came to believe that a Power greater than ourselves could restore us to sanity." Nobody ever seemed to talk about being sane on this Program. They would talk instead about their craziness.

At one meeting back East where I spoke, I talked about being restored to sanity. Someone said to me, "We don't want any of this talk about sanity."

"You don't want to talk about sanity?" I asked.

"No, no," that person said. "It's very dangerous to us. It will destroy our Program."

I said, "I'm sure it will." It certainly will destroy *that* program for those people. In its place there will be a new program. The Twelve Step Program is not supposed to be trudging and horrible, a program of unhappiness. It is a program of sheer joy. God wants us to be happy, not unhappy; to be sane, not crazy; to be thin, not fat; to be sober, not drunk; to be straight, not under the influence of drugs. God wants us to be restored to sanity.

Food is no longer a problem. Food is not my enemy anymore. Food is my friend. I look at an apple and it's beautiful. I go to a bakery every Sunday morning on my way to play tennis, and I pick up sweets for all the other players . . . I love to look at the beautifully decorated cakes in the window display, but I don't eat them.

I have been cured of the necessity of *having* to take that first compulsive bite. That's what Bill W. meant when he said he was cured. I do not eat refined sugar and flour. I don't know why, but physiologically, they are addictive for me.

When it comes to food, my addiciton may not be yours. Some people can handle a piece of bread; it doesn't affect their bodies. If affects mine. Some people binge on meat; I don't care for meat. We all have our own peculiar addictions and compulsions. That's the way it is, and probably that's how it will always be.

You may never be cured of that particular addiction of yours. I don't know whether I will ever be able to eat sugars and flours again. But they are not a problem to me anymore. If someone put a doughnut or a pizza or ice cream in front of me, it would be like a long lost girl friend, an old love . . . "Oh, yes, she was pretty good, but, you know, that was a long time ago."

I can't eat sugar and flour. I also can't run the hundred in nine seconds flat or climb Mt. Kilimanjaro or fly without wings. So what? I accept myself as I am. I will never be cured of being six-foot-one, I'm never going to be six-foot-five. I can make a problem out of it or not.

So I can't eat refined sugars and carbohydrates. That's all right. Do I have to be crazy over it? Not anymore.

God has restored my sanity. There is no person, place, or thing big enough to make me small enough to take that first compulsive bite. It will never happen to me again — not because of my willpower, but because God has relieved me of the compulsion.

God has restored my sanity and I will be sane as long as I am in fit spiritual condition and have absolute faith in my Program of life.

In many ways it is easier to lose two hundred pounds than twenty. When I came to this Program I felt very insecure. I only had, I believed at that time, fifty pounds to lose. I ended up losing over seventy, but I felt very insecure since I didn't have a hundred pounds to lose and somehow that was like a magic number.

There are people around the country now who consider joining the Program not to lose one hundred to two hundred pounds, but to have their sanity restored and be relieved of their compulsion. Periodically, whenever I go to different cities, people come to me and say, "I, too, have been relieved of the compulsion." They write to me and there is a growing list of people who measure the Program not by the amount of weight they have lost but by the restoration of their sanity.

It's incredible what is happening. I know people who have been fighting on the Program three, four, and five years. They've lost weight, put it back on, lost again, and put it on. Then they just stopped worrying about the weight, and when their sanity was restored, the weight came off automatically.

I have met people who have told me that what I say scares them, and I understand that. When you have been fat all your life and come to this Program and lose fifty or a hundred pounds, and someone comes along and says, "That's not all there is," it's scary, all right.

How can you argue with somebody who has — for the first time — lost a hundred pounds? Well, I'm not arguing. But I'm saying that I want *more* than to lose a hundred pounds. I've lost weight lots of times in my life. There are plenty of drunks around who have been dry for long periods of their lives, who will tell you they have licked the problem, and then go right back to drinking.

The program works from the position of faith. As the Big Book says, ". . . We realize that the things which came to us when we put ourselves in God's hands were better than anything we could have planned" (p. 100).

Sponsorship

There are no express or mandatory requirements for sponsors in this Program. The person being sponsored is the sole judge of a sponsor's qualifications. If you have what someone else needs, then it is your duty to serve that person. However, a great deal of self-appraisal is necessary. Remember, we are people who are grandiose and desperate. That applies to both you and the person you sponsor.

A sponsor's duty is to share his or her *recovery* — not to give advice or control anyone by exercising power or by exploiting another person's needs and fear.

Anybody can get up and say things at meetings or be a good speaker. Anybody can lose lots of weight. Anybody who has a few days more abstinence than you looks good. When I first came into the Program I saw people who impressed me and I thought they had serenity. I knew it because they didn't walk, they glided. I thought they had little rollers in their shoes.

But the real test of a sponsor is how he or she lives life. I always tell people to come follow me around before they choose me as their sponsor. Follow me around and see how I am in the real world. Come to my office and see how I deal with business affairs.

Come to my house and see how I act with my family. Watch me drive my car in traffic and shop in stores.

The Big Book of Alcoholics Anonymous discusses only one kind of sponsor — the one who shares how he or she has established a relationship with God. There is no other purpose to sponsorship, nothing else to share. Sponsors are not there in order to give anyone abstinence or sobriety or to get anyone to stop eating compulsively. The only person I can help is myself, and I do that through my Higher Power and through service to others.

It seems to me that the minimum requirement for sponsoring anyone should be *recovery*. Losing weight is not necessarily an indication of recovery, though. Anyone can lose weight by dieting, food-planning, willpower, self-control, discipline, and fear (peer pressure). Losing weight, by itself, is not our problem. Our problem is recognizing that we lack control and that we never will recover control. We recover when we have established a relationship with our Higher Power that enables us to lose weight by having our compulsion removed. This recovery comes about through the Twelve Steps.

The Big Book was written by *recovered* alcoholics. We compulsive overeaters can and will recover, too. Our recovery comes through God, not through a sponsor or any other human power. We recover only by practicing the Twelve Steps in all our affairs and carrying the message of what we learn to other compulsive overeaters through sponsorship. It is not weight loss that is the issue, but the ability to recover sanity through the Higher Power.

In order to find relief from compulsive overeating, we work intensively with other compulsive overeaters. We find a compulsive overeater who *wants* to recover. (We don't waste time trying to persuade anyone who *doesn't* want to recover.) We go to newcomers or prospective newcomers. We do not wait for them to come to us. We ask them two things:

1) whether they *want* to stop compulsive overeating, and
2) whether they will go to *any extreme* to do so.

We tell newcomers that *as part of our own recovery,* we will be glad to talk to them and tell them HOW we recover:

H = Honesty

O = Openmindedness

W = Willingness

We make the Big Book available to them and show them how we substitute the words "compulsive overeater" for "alcoholic," "compulsive overeating" for "alcoholism," "abstinence" for "sobriety," and so on.

We share our experiences and the trouble our compulsion has caused us. We get the newcomer to tell us some of his or her experiences. If his or her mood is light, we tell humorous stories about our overeating and the "games" we played. Then we describe how we came to find out and accept the fact that we had the insanity of overeating. We share the different ways we tried to stop compulsive overeating but could not. We tell the newcomer that we lack the power to control our compulsions. We tell him or her about the mental twist that leads to the first compulsive bite. We explain how the mental condition surrounding the first compulsive bite *prevents* normal functioning of the willpower. If the newcomer sticks to the idea that he or she can still control the compulsion to overeat, we let that person go ahead and try.

If a newcomer is convinced that there is little chance of recovering control on his or her own, we describe the insanity of compulsive overeating. We explain that it is a condition of body (a physical addiction to certain foods which vary according to the person and to large amounts of food) and mind (a mental obsession). We explain that this condition is progressive because it continues to get worse — never better — over time and that it is a fatal illness.

We then let newcomers ask us how we recovered. We tell them exactly what happened to us — that we were willing to believe in a Power greater than ourselves and that we live by spiritual principles (the Twelve Step Program) because living by our own "power" caused us only unhappiness.

We don't talk about religion or theology. We allow others to choose whatever conception they prefer of a Power greater than themselves. We don't try to "instruct" or make demands or list "musts" — we do not play God. We do not play amateur psychologist, either.

If someone asks why his or her religious convictions have not worked and why the spiritual principles of the Twelve Steps work so well, explain that in order for our trust to be vital it must be accompanied by self-sacrifice and unselfish, constructive *action*. "Knowing" is not the same as practicing! We outline the program of action:

1) Tell someone else how you made a self-appraisal, or how you got honest with yourself;

2) Tell someone else how you made restitution for harm done and straightened out your past;

3) Tell someone else *why* you are trying to help others recover — that it is essential to your own recovery, and that anyone who wants to recover must pass the message on to others who want to receive it.

As sponsors, we must realize at all times that the people we sponsor are helping *us* more than we are helping them and let them know this. Realize that the more hopeless and depressed the person you sponsor feels, the more likely he or she will be to be willing to follow the program of *action* — the Twelve Steps.

The person you sponsor will give you "reasons" why he or she "can't" work the Program — why he or she doesn't need *all* of the Program. He or she may rebel at the thought of drastic action such as taking an inventory, discussing it with another person. We admit that we once felt that way but we see we could not have made any progress at all without taking action (working Steps Four through Twelve). Give the person you sponsor time to think it over. He or she must decide for himself or herself.

Newcomers should not be pushed or prodded if they are not interested in our solution. However, we do act as "nurses" for their binges, for they may change their minds after they hurt some more. We carry the message, not the person. The desire for this Program must come from *within.*

If someone thinks he or she can stop overeating some other way or prefers some other approach, encourage that person to follow his or her own way and *let go.* Let him or her know you will still be a friend. If that person leaves, do not be discouraged. Find another compulsive overeater desperate enough to accept with eagerness what we offer. Don't waste time with someone who cannot or will not work with you.

We deprive others of the chance to recover if we spend too much time with one person. We must not let one person impose on us too much. If we permit one person to monopolize our time, we *harm* that person because we make it possible for him or her to be insincere. We may be aiding in that overeater's destruction rather than recovery.

Remember: helping others is the foundation stone of *your* recovery, and "once in a while" isn't enough. You must help someone else every day if need be, at any hour of the day. Remind the people you sponsor that recovery is not dependent upon *people* — you or anyone else. It is dependent upon having a relationship with God. We offer our friendship and fellowship and we will do anything to help others who *want* to get well, but recovery comes through a Higher Power.

Someone who tries to combat compulsive overeating by controlling food with a diet or other means may succeed for awhile, but that person usually winds up going on a bigger binge than ever. We have attempted *all* these methods and we always fail. We never recover control.

As sponsors, we never argue with others about what they are eating or try to keep them from eating. We are careful never to show intolerance or hatred, as an attitude of intolerance might repel someone whose life could have been saved. We can be of little use if we have a bitter or hostile attitude. We have stopped fighting *anybody* or *anything* — even food.

God gives us the power of choice to think through the first compulsive bite to what the consequences may be. This serious and effective thought then gives us the choice over whether to take that first compulsive bite, today and forever.

Remember most of all that your recovery is all you can offer someone else — you are not there to get others to stop overeating, you are there to help yourself. You cannot lose. Whether another person recovers or not, you always win by serving.

When someone says, "I want you to sponsor me," I say, "Fine, let's set a time when you can come and sit for a couple of hours and we'll talk." I don't have any set rules for our talk, but first of all, I want people I sponsor to know that I will never lie, but that I know they will lie to me. They usually say, "I won't lie to you," and I say, "Yes, you will, because that's the first lie." I know it happens and I want them to know that it's perfectly okay. I want them to know they can lie and that I don't care if they lie. I'll know they're lying because I'm an expert at lying myself — we all are. We compulsive overeaters are the most dishonest people I know. We have deceived ourselves all the years of our lives.

We've cheated ourselves out of happiness. Who knows more about cheating than we do? Who knows more about lying to ourselves? We say, "I really look nice today" — and we look like elephants. We look like clowns.

Sometimes I have to tell people I sponsor to go take a bath before we talk. I have to be honest in that way because I know that when I was fat, I was dirty. I didn't want to bathe, and my clothes were dirty. Many of us are that way. So if it is appropriate, I might ask a person to agree to bathe at least once a day. If the person says, "Well, how about once every other day?" I say something like, "I don't care if you don't bathe at all, but you're going to lose a lot of friends." So the first thing people I sponsor get to know is that I won't lie to them.

The second thing I let them know is that I will always be there. I've never told anybody I didn't want to sponsor him or her because of anything that person said or did. I'm always there. "No matter what you do," I say, "even if you don't want to talk to me, fine. If you want to get another sponsor, go get another sponsor. I'll be here whenever you want to come back." Almost invariably, they come back.

My Program — the spiritual principles which guide my life now — is strong enough that nobody threatens it. If somebody threatened my Program, then it wouldn't be a program that anyone would want to learn about or use in the first place. Nobody can take my Program away from me. I can't allow someone else to be more powerful than my commitment to recover from insanity.

The next thing I tell people I sponsor is to eat whatever they want to eat. I don't care what someone else eats. I don't care how others diet. I really want people I sponsor to know that I love them just the way they are, that I don't care if they don't lose an ounce. As a matter of fact, nobody in the world really cares if they lose weight. That's the big lie that we've all been telling ourselves. Actually *we* are the only ones who think there is a problem about our being fat.

The most difficult part of the Program is next. I say, "The hardest thing for you in your relationship with me as a sponsor is that I will never tell you what to do. You never have to do anything."

That really hurts because many people say, "I need a sponsor to tell me what to do. I need people."

I say, "Well, you've got the wrong guy. I'm not going to tell you what to do. I've got enough trouble just dealing with me. I don't know what's good for you. All I can do is share my experience." I can point things out to another person, but if he or she doesn't agree with me, that's okay. I'm not going to disown anyone I sponsor.

One guy used to tell me he wouldn't talk to people he sponsored after they went on binges. Bill W. would still be there all by himself in AA if he had believed that. You can't wait until somebody sobers up before you take him or her into AA. You need a sponsor *after* you binge. A sponsor's not going to stop you from eating, but you need the support and the strength and the love afterwards. No one will put you down as much as you will put yourself down for going on a binge, and *that's* when you need help.

"I'll talk to you anytime," I tell anyone I sponsor. "If you want to go out, I'll even go with you while you eat. It's perfectly okay. I'll have a cup of coffee and hold your hand and I'll be there with you." I've done it. I've gone out with people while they are bingeing.

Once I was at dinner on a retreat and this man was just loading up his plate. Everyone else at the table had taken a quarter of a chicken. He had two quarters and a big salad. I asked, "Are you going to eat that?" Nobody had ever pointed out to him what he was eating. Most people have a code of silence. I don't have any code of silence. I figure if someone points a gun at his head, it's my job to point out that the gun is loaded before he kills himself. So I said to him, "Are you going to eat two quarters of a chicken?" He said, "Yes. Don't take my inventory."

He was going to show me. He went back and got two more quarters. That's what we do. We're going to go out and show everyone. All our lives we have gone around telling the world "I'll show you!" but what we are really saying is "Look at me destroy myself."

We reach a point at which we have to say to ourselves, "Enough is enough. I'm willing to do anything. I'm willing to go to any lengths to stop this insanity." When someone reaches that point, I will make suggestions and say things like, "Don't you think it's time you wrote an inventory?" But I'll never tell anyone what to do.

I find that people often don't hear me when I say that I won't tell them what to do. A young lady I sponsored worked and went to school part time. Like most of us she had a lot of trouble with relationships. She was always in a bad relationship. I was the only one who would tell her they were bad relationships. I say that because she used to say, "Gee, I'm really in love with this guy. I can't live without him." I knew she wanted to be with him out of compulsion, not out of caring. It wasn't the guy. The guys she knew might have been nice guys, but she wouldn't let them be nice guys.

One Friday night she called me up and I knew by the way she talked that she was going out with a loser, so I said so. She asked, "Are you saying that I can't go out with him?"

I said, "No, I won't tell you that you can't go out with him, but I wouldn't go out with anybody who is a loser."

She said, "Well, I can't help it." Those words of hers revealed a lot.

That was Friday and I was going out of town. I asked her if she could wait until Monday before she saw him. She agreed. I returned on Monday, but she didn't call me until Wednesday. She said she was going to get another sponsor. I said okay but asked her to tell me why. She said, "Well, I need a woman sponsor I can relate to." I told her that was all right but that I thought I knew more about her than she herself did. I said I could see she was lying to herself, and it finally came out that she hadn't kept her agreement and had seen the guy she'd told me about.

I said, "So what?" I had known she was going to do that. She wasn't ready to change because she wasn't hurting enough yet. She was just playing around with the Program.

I think it's really sad when people go around saying they are working the Program when all they're really doing is dieting. You aren't working the Program until you give it away — and what have you got to give away if you're just dieting? Losing weight? Anybody can lose weight.

The people I sponsor think I'm terrific because I'm the first one to show them all my faults. They say, "You make mistakes."

I say, "You're absolutely right. I have character defects, and I probably always will." I'm unwilling to get rid of some of those defects, obviously, or I would have gotten rid of them by now. It isn't right or wrong or good or bad, it's just a fact — part of my life doesn't work. When I hurt enough, I'll start working on these defects. Nobody attains perfection.

This is how I deal with the people I sponsor. Sometimes sponsorship is really hard because the temptation most sponsors face is that they want to be parents or dictators. If I lose an ounce and a half more than you or have been in the Program a day more than you, I'm tempted to think I know it all. But if I

work on your life then I don't have to work on my life
— and that's destructive for me.

I have great relationships with the people I sponsor.
I probably get more out of being with them than they
do out of sharing with me. We have tremendous love
and trust for one another.

All of us have to decide why we're going to sponsor
others. Is it in order to be big shots, or in order to save
our own lives and for the sheer joy of helping another
human being?

This anonymous poem is an expression of the
sponsor relationship:

> *You are someone I can talk to,*
> *Someone no one can replace.*
> *You're that someone I can laugh with*
> *Till the tears run down my face.*
> *You're that someone I can turn to*
> *When I need a helping hand.*
> *You're that someone I can count on*
> *To advise and understand.*
> *You're that someone I can sit with*
> *And not need to say a word.*
> *You're that someone I can trust*
> *To keep each confidence you've heard.*
> *You're that someone I think more of*
> *As each day comes to an end.*
> *I'm a very lucky person*
> *To have found such a Special Friend.*

Having Trust

"What would happen if, when you came to the first OA meeting, they talked about God?" The question is often asked. We didn't mention the word in the early days. We thought that talk about God would scare people away. We talked instead about a Higher Power. When a newcomer would ask, "What's a Higher Power?" The answer was, "Whatever you want it to be. Let's say it's the group."

I continued to explain: "If they had talked about God, I probably would have left, because I was an atheist when I came into the Program."

Someone always said, "Aha! There it is! So the reason you stayed around was because they gave you a diet and you lost weight." I said, "That's right, that's the reason I *thought* I stayed around."

If members had approached me the way alcoholics were approached in the Big Book, they could have talked about God all they wanted to.

In these stories, recovered alcoholics came to hospitals and spent hours with alcoholics talking about God and a spiritual program of recovery. They were clear-skinned and dry-eyed, and their hands didn't shake. They had something.

If you are a compulsive overeater at your first meeting, and several people come up to you at a time and talk to you until three in the morning about God, and these people are thin and have clear skin and bright eyes and they talk in self-assured tones without pushing, you would probably say, "I don't know about this God stuff, but they've got something I want!"

Most newcomers come in and are told by a member, "If you want the Program, call me. Here's my number and here's a diet. Stick with it." That's what happened to me. There was no group or individual who sat down with me to explain the Program.

At some meetings, there are greeters who talk to individuals during meeting breaks. They give out their phone numbers. All visitors or newcomers are asked to stand, along with the sponsors. The sponsors' role is explained — to help themselves by serving others. As a sponsor, I say, "I'd like to share my Program with you. May I call you? May I pick you up?" We arrange to meet to spend two or three hours together, and we go through the first three steps.

One person I talked with was very upset with the God part and said, "I can't and I don't accept it."

So I said, "Fine, then don't. Come back when you're ready."

Sometimes I ask, "Do you think you need some more time, or do you want to talk for another hour or two? Or do you want to go out for some coffee?"

Usually the answer is, "Let me think about it, and we'll get together again." Sometimes these people get in touch with me again. Sometimes they don't. I don't chase them if they're not ready.

We used to have retreats where we would add up our weight losses, and we'd have prizes for the table of people that had lost the most weight. We used to think that that was really the important gauge of how the Program worked. Maybe one table had lost 812 pounds — one person had lost 150 pounds and another had lost 200 pounds and another had gained three. But everyone looked good because that table won the prize for the most weight lost. I cheated. I always knew who had lost the most weight, so I always sat at the prize-winning table.

Seldom to this day do we go up to newcomers and tell them that this is a spiritual program, basically because most of us don't believe it ourselves. We like to believe it, but how many of us really trust that God will take away our appetite? He has wars and tragedies and congregations to take care of. Why would He bother with something as unimportant as taking away our appetites?

The reason you hesitate to believe is because you probably have never liked yourself or thought of yourself to be worth enough for God, if He existed, to take away your appetite. When someone professes to believe in God, it's not belief, it's *trust*. *Trust* is the key word. If you really *trust* that God *is*, then, of course, you will work those steps. Otherwise, you may never work them because they're not easy. Who wants to make amends to a bunch of characters out there who probably deserve what you did to them in the first place? Or you might not want to give up a character defect like lying. You may not even know what truth is anymore!

We go through the pain and discomfort of this Program, because of a promise at the end that God is going to take away our appetites.

We don't see much visual proof. Where are all these people whom the Program has already worked for? There were people around who appeared to be working a successful Program because they lost weight. But those who lost put it back on if their Programs were based only upon a foundation of food and diets.

Since we all felt that food was our problem, all we talked about was food. Conventions were held around whether we should eat this or eat that. Food sponsors played God: they told you what to eat and whom to date. Since some people's interpretation of the Program was based on a false premise, naturally some people failed.

For me, I needed proof. How could I trust without proof? The few times in my life that I have trusted, I got a kick in the pants or a stab in the back. If there was really a God, how come I had this miserable life? How come I was fat?

The only reason I am here today is because I finally found the success of the Program and I found it through alcoholics and AA's Big Book. Their stories held out to me the proof I had been looking for.

I've never been an alcoholic, but I went to AA meetings. I found some old timers in AA who had been in the Program for twenty, thirty, or forty years, and they were different. A lot of these old timers really do live a spiritual life.

There's not one of you who hasn't dieted and hasn't lost weight, but probably you have not kept it off for long periods of time. Just as alcoholics can stop drinking, we can stop eating compulsively in many ways and in many places. We can wire our mouths. We can undergo bypass surgery. We can go on diets. There are all kinds of ways whereby we can stop eating and lose weight. Most of them fail in the long run.

It's so hard for me to convince you to give up those weight-losing methods. It is so difficult to let go of a diet, to sit back and have trust that another way is going to work.

There is another way — a Program of recovery. It is set forth in the Big Book of Alcoholics Anonymous. Please realize that the Big Book was written by recovered people. By "recovered," they meant that their compulsion to drink was taken away. That doesn't mean that some of them didn't think of drinking sometimes. Many of them did. I think about eating at times, even now, but not one tenth as often as I did. What is more important is that I don't have to act on my compulsion.

When I am obsessed with food, that lets me know that I'm not living the Twelve Step Program all the time. The degree that I live the Twelve Step Program is the degree to which my obsession is removed.

You've got to believe that you can recover. If you don't believe it, you are wasting your time. There isn't a one of us who hasn't felt at times recovered. Who, for one moment, has not felt full and happy with yourself? Now you recall, "Yes, I do remember those times I really had no appetite."

That feeling could happen to you most of the time. How do we know these compulsions can disappear? Through the stories of the AA members in the Big Book.

Compulsive overeaters may have trouble finding people who live a spiritual life, for whom the compulsion of food has been removed. Why? Because we've never been taught much about this kind of Program in the first pace.

To show others who are still drinking precisely how alcoholics have recovered is the main purpose of the Big Book. To show other compulsive overeaters precisely how I and others have recovered is my goal in life and the purpose of this book.

The Big Book says that these alcoholics hope that their message will prove so convincing that no further authentication will be necessary. When I read this, there were very few recovered overeaters around for me to look to as role models, that is, very few thin ones who had kept their weight off for any length of time.

When I read the Big Book, I was willing to believe that these AA members could authenticate the Twelve Step recovery Program. I read and reread the stories. I got to know the people in them until they became old friends. I could visualize how they looked, where they lived, what they did. Since then, I've met two of the people who wrote stories in the Big Book and they are exactly as I had fantasized.

Many people outside the Program do not comprehend that the alcoholic or the compulsive overeater is a very sick person. However, we know that we're very sick people.

When I originally read the Big Book I didn't relate much to alcoholics and their recovery. But when I learned that their way of living has advantages for all, I knew there was a path for me.

The only requirement to join the Twelve Step Program was an honest desire to stop drinking (or eating compulsively). Now that sounds simple until you start to look at it. I didn't understand the meaning of the word "honest." At the very most I thought honesty meant not lying to others, but the real concept means being honest with yourself. That was hard. I had to live with me. I might be able to delude others, but every time I looked in the mirror, I saw me — the living proof of failure. I didn't want to stop eating compulsively. What I really wanted was to be thin and eat the way I always had. We all want that.

How I played the food game! One Twinkie won't hurt me. How much can a Twinkie weigh? I would ask myself. I would answer that one Twinkie is not going to retard my weight loss. So I would eat one. Not only did I not gain weight, I lost two pounds that day. If I lost two pounds with one Twinkie, I decided I would have two Twinkies. Maybe I'd lose four pounds.

Then one day I didn't have any Twinkies and I gained. Since I didn't understand my body metabolism, I started fooling around with it. That may sound funny, but it's no different than plotting and figuring what you're going to eat, whether it's counting Twinkies or weighing and measuring other foods.

We think we are going to be able to discipline ourselves, but we haven't ever been able to do that. Why? I really had to think about that. The answer? I wanted to stop being fat, but I had no desire at all to stop eating.

It took me a long time to get past those words about honesty in the Big Book, because that was the requirement for membership. Nobody threw me out of a meeting, of course, but I had to live with myself. I had to decide whether 1) I could acquire this honesty, and 2) I really wanted to stop eating.

We tell ourselves not to worry about "forever," just one day at a time. But for me now *is* forever. I am never going to be able to have a sandwich, or other common foods others eat all the time. I have to ask, "Is it worth it?"

Anyone who decides that he or she wants this Program has to recognize that this is the way it is. The alcoholic doesn't say, "Well, I'm just not going to drink for today. Tomorrow I might be able to drink." The alcoholic may be able to deal with it for just a day at a time, but it is, in fact, forever. Finally the day came that, for one day at a time, I was willing to stop eating those things forever. I didn't know how I would feel tomorrow or next week, but for today I was willing to stop eating those things forever.

I was willing because the pain was terrible. Only if the pain of where you are is worse than the fear of where you are going will you be willing to surrender and begin working the Program. If you're not willing, if you don't have an honest desire to stop eating compulsively, then you are fooling yourself. Lots of people come to the Program for the convenience of losing a couple of pounds. But, if it is to work, this is a Program that comes out of pain. Only when I hurt, and the pain of being fat became unbearable, was I willing to go to such lengths.

The day finally came when I said, "I don't know whether I will ever again tell a lie to anyone else, but I can't lie to myself anymore. It's just too painful. I'm willing now, just for today, to stop eating those things forever. Just for today, I'm willing to commit myself to turn the problem over to whatever figment of Higher Power there may be. I will not eat compulsively those things that make me fat."

Now it's been years since I have eaten those fattening foods. "One day at a time" is right — but each day I know that tomorrow will not allow me to eat bread or any of those other foods that make me fat.

The foreword to the second edition of the Big Book told me how the Program works through others. Compulsive overeaters' sharing with each other is vital to permanent recovery. They didn't say just recovery; they said permanent recovery. That really excited me and made me hopeful.

The Big Book also talked about fellowship. There seemed to be a lot of caring and affection — but also a lot of people seemed to be telling everybody else what to do when they weren't doing it themselves. I was probably more guilty of this than anyone else. If I told you what to do, I didn't have to tell *me* what to do. As long as I played God with you, I didn't have to find a God for myself. That worked for a while until people began to see through me.

I was once at a meeting place in Texas where they have a twenty-four-hour AA meeting hall with a stage. On each side of the stage, they had these gigantic life-size pictures — must be six feet tall — of Bill W. and Dr. Bob. I knew if those men were alive today, they'd be sick over such deification.

We compulsive overeaters do that, too. We find somebody who is thin or who is able to verbalize the Program's success and we deify that person.

Bill W. and Dr. Bob didn't need deification; all they needed was to stay sober. You have to realize how selfish they had to be to maintain their own sobriety. They went out helping all those other still-drinking alcoholics who thought they were doing it for *them.* But they were really helping themselves. When I go to speak at Program retreats and meetings, I have the compulsion taken away, just the way they did.

Bill W. was a brilliant, righteous, angry, disciplined individual with an incredible ego. If the Program worked for him, it can work for any of us. When you come in to the Program helpless, out of work, with no family, it's easier to accept the problem and the

Program. Bill W. was not helpless. He had lost and made a lot of money, but basically he was still able to make a good living, and his family was still with him.

What happened to him was that he met a recovered alcoholic and said to himself, "I want what this man has."

He was relieved to learn that every alcoholic's will is amazingly weak when it comes to resisting alcohol. Our wills are amazingly weak when it comes to resisting food, even though we often remain strong in other respects. My overeating behavior in the face of a desperate desire to stop was unexplainable. We eat even though we want to stop eating! When we figure out ways we're going to stop eating . . . that's called dieting. We count calories. We figure what we can or can't eat. But each one of us has a unique body chemistry. What's good or non-fattening for you is not necessarily good or non-fattening for me. We are the last persons in the world who can determine what's good for us to eat. Can you imagine an addict figuring out when or when not to use coke, or who can or can't use heroin? It's ludicrous. What alcoholic would be in a position to determine what proof or what label of alcohol is all right to drink and what isn't? Alcoholics can't deal with alcohol any more than we can deal with food.

The miracle is that, in this Program, we never have to deal with food. What can happen to us is exactly what happened to Bill. W. When he looked up a friend from the Oxford Group, did the man say, "You must start tapering off," or "Bill, you must start calling in your alcohol to me everyday?" No. This man made a point-blank declaration that God had done for him what he could not do for himself. Now why did Bill W., this sophisticated, urban stockbroker, buy this idea? Because the pain of his drinking was worse than the fear of not drinking. The pain was bad enough that he was willing to believe that God would do for him what he could not do for himself.

Bill W. asked the man what kind of God he had found and how to find a God. The man suggested he choose his own concept of God. Bill W. admitted that this idea hit him hard. In the Big Book he says, "It melted the icy intellectual mountain in whose shadow I had lived and shivered many years . . . It was only a matter of being willing to believe in a Power greater than myself. Nothing more was required of me to make my beginning. I saw that growth could start from that point . . . Upon a foundation of complete willingness I might build what I saw in my friend" (p. 12).

Bill W. continued, "I humbly offered myself to God, as I then understood Him, to do with me as He would." That means that we offer ourself to a Higher Power, this God of our choosing, without conditions, not upon conditions that we lose weight.

A person might say, "Okay, Bill, I'll try it out. I'll give it a test; I'll put my foot in the water. If the water's not warm, or if I'm not going to be able to walk on it, I'm not going in." We say to ourselves, okay, we're going to believe in God, but we want to see the proof in ourselves. If we don't lose the weight overnight, forget it. That's why we need role models, the people for whom this Program has worked.

Our Program begins not when we start losing weight, but when we help another person. That is sobriety. That is abstinence. Abstinence has nothing to do with losing weight, but rather with abstaining from an insane way of life. Losing weight comes automatically as a by-product of a certain kind of life. Alcoholics Anonymous was not founded by one man when he became sober. It came into being when he helped another person and that man became sober.

Someone who claims to have been on the Program for two years usually means he or she has been dieting for two years. "Being on the Program" means living the Twelve Steps by helping another person. That's living the Program. Does it mean going out and helping fat people? Yes. Does it mean going out and being nice to other people? Yes. It even means helping people we don't like — *especially* people we don't like. It means practicing these principles in all our affairs, as Step Twelve says.

The more uncomfortable it is to live this Program, the more valuable it is. When you live with a parent, a child, or a spouse who knows how to press your buttons to make you react, refuse to have buttons to press. God takes away your vulnerability. God can't take that away if you avoid people or situations, if you're afraid of them, or if you give them the power over you. You must face your problems. This is easier said than done, but it is possible. Just start with faith in God and trust that you can change.

I Don't Hear the Words

There's a saying that goes something like this: "I'm so busy looking at what you do that I don't hear the words." I like that because often that's the way it is in the Program.

All of us have heard speakers at meetings. Sometimes we judge what we get from these speakers by their speech-making abilities. This one was funny. That one made you cry. Another was a master of beautiful language. Yet the value of any speaker is not in the actual words used, but in the message conveyed.

The most value I can offer people as a speaker is that though perhaps they did not understand every word I said, they can walk away knowing that what they have heard may help them to move on and grow in their lives. It gives me great happiness when a year or two after an appearance, I meet someone who says, "I heard you speak at such-and-such a place. I didn't understand exactly what you were talking about, but somehow what you said was a catalyst for change in my life."

In the Program, we hope that we can get our message across by example. We become examples that somebody, somewhere can relate to and say, "I don't understand all the words. But that person has what I want — so I'll do what he (or she) did."

In the Big Book on page 189, there is a story about two of the AA founders who went to a hospital and talked to an alcoholic. The alcoholic began to have new hope, thinking "If they can do it, I can do it." In one evening, you can judge the effectiveness of a person's Program, as this alcoholic did. Even though he may have resented his visitors' attitude, he understood that, after a life similar to his own or worse, these men were no longer drinking. The alcoholic wanted that for himself.

As a compulsive overeater, you want the Program a speaker has to offer — not the words.

To a person who is unfamiliar with the steps, our Program may sound full of paradoxes, even ridiculous. But it works, not only to stop compulsive eating, but as a way of life.

We have been told all our lives that self-control is what we need in order to lose weight. Now the very first thing we are told in the Program is that we can't control ourselves, that we need to give up our attempt to control everything. That is a paradox in itself. We want to lead happier lives, and we are told that the way to do it is to stop trying.

The Twelfth Step seems like a paradox, too. When you give away your Program and your way of life, that is how you keep it for yourself.

We help each other by being examples ourselves. My sharing something of value is important to you, as well as to me. It is essential for my life that you get value out of my sharing because that, after all, is the seal of approval on my Program. If, when I see you at some later time, you say, "You know, I heard you speak, and that helped me in my life," your endorsement is assurance to me that I am working the right kind of a Program.

We all look for reasons why we eat. I was the kind of eater who never ate much during the day. Nor was I a big-meal eater. But I ate constantly from the time I got home in the evening until I went to sleep.

Each of us overeats differently. Some are sweet eaters. Some go out in the middle of the night to eat. Regardless of the differences in the specific eating behaviors that make us fat, the real reason we are fat is very simple: we eat too much.

A woman once told me that she was not a compulsive overeater because she almost never ate. She said she was a selective, compulsive overeater. I was selective, too: I would select anything that was available!

We all say that we want to learn how to stop eating so much, but actually we don't really want to stop eating too much, we just want to be thin. If we could just have a magic formula whereby we could keep on eating and also be thin, we would pay a fortune for it. But unfortunately there is no such formula.

I spent years arguing with the facts of life. I could argue that a tree was not a tree, if I wanted it to be something else. I did not want to recognize the fact that some people can eat more than others and not get fat. After arguing for years about the unfairness of life,

I had to conclude that if I ate as much as I wanted to eat, *I got fat.* What others could or could not eat didn't matter.

The foreword to the Big Book says that this Program has advantages for everybody, not only for alcoholics. In order to attain happiness through the Program, you don't have to start from being crazy, from being two hundred pounds overweight, from being a heroin addict or a drunk in a jail cell, or from being destitute after gambling away your life's savings.

I know that I no longer eat compulsively or worry about food. I believe I have been restored to sanity, as the Program promises, and I will stay sane as long as I work the Program "in all my affairs." The Big Book also says that "half measures avail us nothing." So I believe, too, that unless I am willing to work this Program every day to the best of my ability in all my affairs, then I am not working it at all. I can't work it only to lose weight. Besides, happiness does not come just from losing weight. I can guarantee that when I lost weight, nothing else changed until I was willing to accept myself.

If you are looking for examples, you can't love people who don't love themselves. You can't follow the Program of those who don't work the Program themselves. You can't judge a person's Program by the pounds lost, since there are plenty of skinny, crazy people around, along with a lot of fat, sane ones. The quality of your life is the quality of your Program (and vice versa) — not simply how thin you are.

I have learned to like myself, even though I'm not perfect. Still, we strive for physical, emotional, and spiritual perfection on this Program. It's not important whether we reach it. My goal every day is to find oneness with my God, oneness with the people I meet in the Program and in my daily life.

Don't judge me only on what I say, because it's easy to talk. I have heard speakers give fantastic talks, and when I actually saw them in private life, I didn't want anything they had.

I have told those who wanted me to be their sponsor to follow me through a day, see me in my everyday life, see that I'm no god; I'm not even a perfect human being. I have a lot of faults, which I am willing to acknowledge. I am also willing to acknowledge my good points.

I don't eat compulsively. I live what I consider a spiritual life. I value my relationship with my Higher Power. I know how to love people. And in any given day, I am ten times happier than I ever used to be. If, through some accident or physical quirk I gained one hundred pounds tomorrow, I would still love myself although I would question what I had done to abuse my body.

I can find unhappiness anytime I want — and sometimes I still do. But I handle it differently now. I work my Program, allowing myself to be just the way I am, and allowing others to be just the way they are. I have found a new life for myself in this Program.

Get the Big Book and read it. Put it under your pillow; maybe you'll get its message by osmosis. The

Big Book espouses a way of life that I believe has been God-given.

If you work the Program, you are going to lose weight. That's all there is to it.

When you look up to successful weight losers in the Program, don't just listen to what they are saying at meetings. Follow them around. See how they lead their lives. See if they have what you want — not just thinness, but a Program of living that you want to emulate.

Would you tell your child that you want him (or her) to be like you? I will tell my children that, yes, I want them to be like me, because I like me now. I would not have said that several years ago. Now I want my children to be like me because I have something of value for them. I have a way of life that this Program has given me.

Switching Compulsions

My compulsive overeating is primarily mental. I can be fat without gaining an ounce. I remember once my wife and I were looking at a picture of her in her early teens and she said, "My, I was ugly." But she said she had never realized it because her parents kept telling her how beautiful she was. As a teenager, she had a great personality and plenty of friends. She was not aware that she was going through an awkward, homely stage.

Many of us are unaware that we're fat unless we *believe* we're fat. Sometimes when I get up in the morning, I feel fat. This has nothing to do with my body; it has to do with my Program.

I used to wake up unhappy and blame my unhappiness on everybody else. If it was cloudy day, I'd say, "I just know I'm going to be miserable!" And, sure enough, I'd become miserable and depressed.

Now if it's a cloudy day when I wake up, I say, "Look at the formation of those clouds!" I enjoy everything about the whole day, even the clouds.

Before, if I had a problem and I felt uncomfortable in the morning, I'd have to find out *why* I was uncomfortable and be constantly trying to get rid of the problem.

I always had to find a reason behind my discomfort. Some of us say, "I don't feel good today and it's your fault." Or you blame your feeling rotten on the kids, the job, your husband, the traffic, or the weather.

As a big sports fan, I'd be depressed when the local team lost. My depression lasted for a few minutes and then I'd get on with my day. Conversely, if they won I'd feel terrific. I had given the team the power to make me feel bad or good. This is a small, harmless example. Most of us are not aware that we do not have to allow *anything* or *anyone* out there to have the power to make us feel bad or good.

What we say is "I feel depressed." But instead of just saying, "So what?" we go on and ruin our day. Since we are masters at rationalization, it requires only a few seconds to come up with something we can use as a reason for our feeling terrible — a place to go where we don't want to be, a bill we have to pay, a car that needs repair. Although nothing in the world has the power to make us feel rotten unless we give it the power, we can find a million and one excuses for feeling bad.

We call up a friend and complain, looking for validation for our bad feelings. That person may support us in our bad feelings, "Oh yes, isn't that awful!" When others agree with us, that seems to validate our insanity.

Most people don't want to hear the truth. They would rather hear support for their bad feelings. What happens is that we support each other inappropriately.

I can either go ahead about the day's business and be slightly depressed, or I can really wallow in my depression. The point is that I have made it so far through my life surviving traumas, doing what I had to do one way or the other.

I will survive tomorrow, too — one of these days I'm going to be eighty-five years old and I'm going to look back and say, "Whew! I made it."

We will all play out the game, rich or poor, fat or thin. We are all going to die. That's all there is to it. The game will be over and the only difference there is between any of us is the amount of time we have spent each day in happiness.

Do people really change compulsions? Probably not. They become more sophisticated perhaps. That's what switching compulsions really is — just more mind games. I read about an alcoholic who had been dry for eighteen years and had never really worked the Program. "What have I proved?" he asked himself. He wasn't drunk anymore, but instead he was angry, hostile, and depressed. As he stopped boozing, he switched over to getting high on anger and low on depression in order to again prevent himself from living and enjoying life. He found that drinking to give himself a downer had been easier. Now that he was no longer drinking, he had to avoid life and happiness in more sophisticated, less obvious, and more subtle ways.

We are all different in our makeup. I certainly never wished to be a compulsive overeater. I'd love to be able to go out and eat whatever I want. I have a son who eats like a horse and never gains an ounce. When I ask him how things are going, he'll say, "Fine, but I just can't seem to put on any weight." Well, God made me my way and God made him his way, and I don't know why.

Some days I feel fat in my head. But I know that when I feel unhappy or fat, if I act as if I am not and don't fight it, in a while the feeling will end. If I just wait it out, the feeling really will go away provided I don't act on my unhappy feelings.

When we stop drinking or overeating, we become more sophisticated and subtle, and sometimes we switch compulsions. Since we are not drinking or overeating, we appear to be working the Program.

You see, what happens is that every time we get to the crucial point in our programs when we begin to change, when we make a big breakthrough, we often resist and backtrack. We binge, refuse to lose those last few pounds, or yo-yo.

Then finally comes the moment for all of us — that last big break when we say good-bye to our former selves, our bondage, and our compulsions. You'll know when you're going through this final change because there's a certain feeling you will have — like saying good-bye to an old love, which is what it really is.

In our crazy past insanity, we were only able to cope, instead of really live. When we begin to fully live life, we have to say good-bye to that old way of simply coping. When our craziness has no more value or use for us, a real feeling of sadness can come over us. You used to really get excited when you went to a party. Now you say to yourself, "How come I'm not so excited anymore by all this? How come the things that used to really turn me on don't anymore?"

After the sadness comes a void, a nothingness. What used to excite you no longer does.

This is the crucial point: You are going to go back and hook into your past craziness, or you're going to switch compulsions — or, hopefully, you're going to pass through this phase, filling the void with healthy activities. When you pass through it, that's when the Program starts working. You see, being sane is a heck of a lot of work. It never ends.

The day you become complacent, perhaps twenty-five years from now, and say, "I've kept my weight off twenty-five years now, I don't have to work on happiness anymore" — *whacko!* — one day is all it would take and you could be right back where you started.

We find it too easy to lie to ourselves and switch compulsions — that is, to switch the game we play. Somebody once asked me about diet drinks and gum, "Isn't it just as much a compulsion now that, instead of eating, I drink all those diet drinks and chew a lot of gum?"

I said, "You have substituted one compulsion for another. You have to sit with the feeling of not moving your mouth, whether it's to drink or eat or chew gum or whatever."

If we leave that unhappy void there, we will be open to switching compulsions. Several years ago, after I had been abstaining for quite a while, I thought I was going to binge in the middle of the night, and I went down to the refrigerator. I said to myself, "This is it — I'm hungry and I'm going to eat." I sat on the floor in front of the open refrigerator and looked at all that food and I said, "You are really a dummy. You finally lost all your extra weight and you have everything in the world you want — a great Program, a terrific family, good friends, enough money to live on and no real problems. And what you really want to do most in the world is eat! You know it's going to kill you."

I got up and found a piece of paper and pencil and I started making a fantasy list of all the things in the world I would like to do now or ever thought I would like to do. To this list, I added what I thought any normal, sane, healthy person liked to do for fun. I even put down some things people did for fun that I didn't like to do — like scuba diving.

I looked over my list and realized that I hadn't done many of those things. I had chosen to eat and be fat instead. It was so much easier.

When people that I sponsor come to me, I ask, "What do you do for yourself to give yourself fun?" They think and think and then they admit they don't know, and that's the truth.

We seldom think we are worth treating ourselves to happiness. We do things in conjunction with other people to make them happy, and we lose the ability to be individual human beings.

After putting everything I could think of on my midnight list, I crossed off the activities that I considered impossible — like making love to Sophia Loren. I mean, that just wasn't going to happen, but still it was a good fantasy!

Then I went through the list again and crossed off three or four things that I absolutely did not want to do. Finally, I picked out six that were possible or that I had tried before. I made up my mind I was going to do all of them. I was going to live, be happy, and get off food. It didn't matter if I liked the activity or not. I would do it anyway and keep doing it.

When I took up tennis, I didn't like it. I thought it was the stupidest sport I'd ever seen — walking around in those little shorts and hitting some dumb little ball. I hated it so much that I would tell myself I didn't have the time for it or sabotage myself so I wouldn't enjoy it. I would arrange lessons and forget about them and the pro would call up and say, "Where were you at four o'clock?" But I kept playing tennis because I knew that unless I got out there and seized life and filled that void with good healthy activities, I was going to fill it with bad feelings one way or the other.

I stayed at tennis for years, and finally I can now say that tennis for me is as much fun — even more fun than eating ever was. And I used to think that nothing ever could replace the fun that eating was for me. But tennis does, and skiing could. Even scuba diving could.

I wanted to race cars, and I found an oval track where you can go and pay and drive around it like a race driver. I did it.

I did all kinds of things I never thought I could do physically or never could afford to do. If your fantasy is going to France, you can start putting away ten dollars a month now. Begin to plan and don't forget that the trip starts now with all the fun of anticipation. It's not just putting the money away, because every month when you put the ten dollars away, for those few brief moments you're already in France.

Don't sabotage yourself by figuring out ways *not* to enjoy life. Don't live a life of futility crowded with bad feelings. Being thin will be a battle for you unless you are willing to allow your life to be turned around and filled up with good feelings.

I still have to make a concerted effort to give myself happiness, to enjoy life. Whenever I say, "Oh, I don't want to do that" or "It's too much trouble" or "I'm afraid to do that," then I have one foot in the door to going right back where I came from — just feeling bad instead of living life and enjoying it.

I have a foot on a banana peel, ready to slip right back if I allow any guilt, frustrations or anxieties to sway me, through rationalizations, from my purpose of enjoying life.

I just don't believe God put any of us on this earth to be miserable. I am defeating His will and purpose if I persist in ways of living that make me miserable and unhappy.

When I talk about enjoying life, I don't mean momentary fun for which you're going to pay a dear price later. You could say that eating for us might be fun — for a moment. I don't mean substitutes for our compulsions either. And don't find a way to make a problem out of a pleasure. Enjoying yourself should not be a problem.

Make this activity list to free yourself, to really get out there and live life for *you*. All those excuses like "I don't have time" or "I don't have the money" are ridiculous. You're never too old for fun! I know lots of people seventy years or older who are getting out and enjoying life. I'm talking about individual fulfillment, not just what you could do easily like going to the movies, but what other active people have always done for fun. Don't just try these things. Do them hundreds of times and get good at them.

You have been getting your excitement from compulsive eating and from other compulsive people. Another compulsion is getting into bad relationships. Going out with someone who is rotten or mean provides you a lot of excitement. You know, if there were a thousand people in the room, any one of us would probably navigate to the one alcoholic or compulsive overeater or gambler in the crowd.

First of all, we are afraid to risk being alone. We get hooked into lousy relationships, and we would rather have a lousy relationship than none. We'd rather feel bad than not feel at all. What we don't understand is that we have the option to feel good.

You only have one shot at life. I don't know if the world is going to end fifty years from now. I don't know for certain if there is a hereafter. But I do know I have been given this life, and I'm going to make the most of it. I am not going to get caught up in bad relationships anymore.

If you are married to someone who is crazy or sick — say he is a drunk who will not go to AA — accept the fact that he has been that way for twenty years, and he probably is not going to change. Stop blaming your unhappiness on him, because he is truly not the cause of it. He does not have to be the cause of the way you feel, so stop being the effect of him. You can go out and have a happy life no matter who your spouse is or who your parents or your children are. They cannot cause your unhappiness in any way unless you allow them to.

You can make bad relationships or money into problems for yourself, just as you make food a problem. Stop making everything and everybody out there your god. You are a human being. Stop being a wind-up toy and letting external things make you react in ways that always bring you unhappiness. One of the worst compulsions is to plug into someone else's insanity and allow that to be the cause of how you feel. Stop giving others the ability to wind you up and send you where you don't really want to be and make you who you really are not.

Right now you have to start living. If you don't learn that from this Program, I don't know where you're going to find it. There are promises everywhere for a happy life, but this Program is the only way of life I've ever found that really gave it to me.

You have to do the footwork and the inventory, make the amends, seek contact with a Higher Power, as if your life depended on it — which it literally does. You are going to find more and more subtle ways to lie to yourself if you do not really work this Program. You will find more sophisticated ways of being crazy which you won't even recognize as such unless you are totally committed to this Program.

Very seldom do I see people move more than a fraction in the direction of real change. You may look as if you've changed, but the way to know if you have really changed is to ask yourself, "How many hours a day do I spend in happiness?" That is a genuine criterion of change.

Being thin only gives me a few seconds of happiness when I wake up and look in the mirror in the morning. I say, "Oh, yeah, I'm thin." That's about it. No real, lasting happiness; being thin gives me just two minutes more in happiness each day than I used to have. The world doesn't stop turning just because I lost some pounds. Traffic doesn't stop for me just because I'm thin. Satellites don't beep forth the news, "Bill has lost weight." No, nothing has changed out there.

For a long time I didn't change either. I was just a fat person in a thin body waiting to get fat again. My head was still choosing to give myself unhappiness and unwilling to fill in that void and just waiting to get back there to my fat old ways of doing things.

Unless you are totally committed and are willing to give yourself happiness, you are never going to change. You will be that same insane person and you will go back to making food a problem for yourself, along with other compulsions I have mentioned.

No matter how ridiculous you think it seems, work this Program just for you. Do it without fear. Do it with trust that it works. It is never too late to begin.

Go out and enjoy life. Begin by making the list of things to do for fun, commit yourself to doing some of those things for yourself — not for your husband, parents, or children, but just for you.

Once you've conquered one activity, start another, and once you've conquered that, take up another and stay at it. If other people like roller skating, there must be some fun about roller skating, for example, and if *you* don't like it there must be something wrong with you, so keep at it until you go sane roller skating — or whatever it is you decide to undertake.

I took up roller skating, and then I took up ice skating and skiing. Believe me, I looked like a teddy bear bundled up coming down the mountain! Now I love skiing. I go to the mountain and say, "Well, that's about a six-fall hill!" I'm never going to be a great skier, but if I just take four falls I'm a success! I don't need to be an expert to enjoy it.

I never thought I'd go bike riding, either. Now I go out and ride along a twenty-mile bike path by the ocean. I don't do this for the kids or my wife. I do it for me. I'm not denying my God-given life anymore.

If you don't live for yourself, you are going to find yourself switching from a food compulsion to other compulsions that are real dead-ends and can never give you happiness. Happiness is always a by-product of work, a gift that comes indirectly.

In our insanity we think we can go after pleasure directly, and we always mess it up by indulging. If we're left up to our old devices and choices, we give ourselves bad trips. It requires great effort to break away from those old ways that did not work — nor will they ever work. If you are still switching compulsions, you are not working this Program. You have to substitute living life for your compulsions — and the Twelve Step program will show you how.

Anger

The Big Book says, "If we are to live, we have to be free of anger. Anger and resentments are not for us. They are the dubious luxuries of normal men, but for the alcoholic (or the compulsive overeater) these things are poison." How can we avoid being angry with others? How can we recognize that when someone is being offensive, he is spiritually sick, and we then have to be tolerant and patient?

Dealing with anger and resentment is one of the hardest things in the world. For a long time, I would not acknowledge that I had any angers or resentments. I was not the kind of person who showed any anger. I never really allowed my feelings to show — and certainly not my anger.

To be angry with you was to acknowledge that you bothered me, and I was not going to admit that you affected me at all. What I found out was that I set myself up to be stepped on, so then I could say that I was just a nice guy who never got angry. What I was really saying was, "Please step on me."

After a while I realized that, instead of either holding in my anger or beating somebody up, there was another way. *That was to experience my anger or resentment and then let it be.* I could recognize my feelings, but I didn't have to act on them.

We compulsive overeaters seem to think that we always have to act, to do something. We have trouble letting things alone. When I was eating compulsively, if there was a crumb of cake on a plate, I couldn't leave it alone. I couldn't throw it out. Throwing out a piece of cake is like losing an arm! It's like death! Sometimes I will still stop off at a place and buy something to eat, compulsively. I sit with it untouched and then go to a garbage can and throw it away. It tears me apart.

To sit with feelings of anger and resentment and *not* do something about them is an almost impossible ordeal. That's part of our insanity, our disease, that we are "fixers" and doers.

Did you ever tell a nagging or overprotective parent, "Why don't you just leave the kid alone?" That parent has to manipulate the children's entire lives. If you, as a parent or anyone else, recognize that someone is doing this — or anything else you consider wrong — you find it difficult to just leave the matter alone and not engage in what I call righteous or justifiable interference. We compulsive types, again, need to "do something."

Giving up angers and resentments can be a horrendous experience. Not to *have* to get angry when somebody does something you resent makes for a great void in your life. You will find as you deal with each one of your character defects that, as it is removed, it leaves a void, an emptiness. It's like an old friend passing away. That defect is like the last string bean on a plate that you just leave there, like the last drink put before the alcoholic and turned down.

What do I do now without my angers? We all are afraid of that feeling of emptiness, which leaves us feeling anxious and unprotected. Say, for example, a relative who has been doing the same annoying thing all your life does it once again. Only this time you give up and say, "I'm not going to be angry about that anymore." What do you do instead?

When your children announce that they are running away from home and you say, "Go ahead," instead of getting angry, what else is there to talk about?

Your husband threatens you one time too many, and now you don't get angry. Now what? You don't eat over it. (That has always been your option before.) You don't yell and scream over it. What do you do?

That's where the spiritual part of our Program comes in. Until you get to that point, you do not have a place to go. What happens is that all of a sudden you cease to have extreme highs or lows of emotions. Things steady down.

Suddenly you may say, "It just dawned on me — that son-of-a-gun made that remark to me two weeks ago and I forgot to get angry."

Your "righteous anger" has disappeared. In its place are the routines and joys of life — such mundane considerations as making a good living instead of a lousy one, having good relationships instead of going out with the usual jerks, playing tennis, riding bicycles, jogging, going to the theater. All those good alternatives to overeating.

My so-called fun in life — besides sitting in front of the television and munching — had always been negative. I either found it by acting out my anger or withholding it in resentments. Usually what I resented in others were behaviors that I also saw in myself or that I envied.

I most resented people who did not have to go to the lengths I had to go to in order to overcome my compulsions. Only recently have I been able to get rid of my resentments of those on the Program who binge. How can they binge and get away with it? They are alive, but I know that if I binge, a part of me is going to die.

I resented people who had more popularity than I did. I resented people who seemed not to care if I liked them or not.

When you allow God to remove your resentments, you begin to look at those people you once resented in a new light. God has a funny way of playing tricks on me; sometimes a person I resent turns out to be particularly nice.

I now acknowledge that I have had resentments. I also acknowledge that they are totally debilitating to me. They prevent me from working much of a Program in my life. Yet when I got rid of my angers and resentments, I was bored without them. I was like an empty vessel waiting for something to fill the emptiness.

The feeling that seems to be behind all others is fear. When you see angry and resentful people, they are covering up fears. I don't believe people who tell me they are not afraid of anything. I know they carry a lot of angers and resentments. Compulsive overeating, crazy ideas about sex, money mismanagement — these are all real problems. The main underlying problem, however, is fear.

Some ask if there are differences between anger and resentment and hatred. To me, they are the same. Just the degree varies.

Usually I hate people that are safe to hate — Hitler, for instance. We seldom acknowledge our hate feelings. Sometimes we hate our parents, teachers, spouses, and even our children. Those feelings are okay to have. But what you do with those feelings determines their appropriateness and indicates the extent of your maturity.

I can honestly say that I am almost, though not completely, devoid of anger and resentment. Our real angers and resentments are not often from what others do, but from the frustrations of our own lives.

The bottom line is that we want to control our environment. We want to control the world — our kids, the sun, the moon, food, and, of course, our weight. We want to be God. Our biggest fears are of being manipulated, of being out of control. When you are dead, you are no longer in charge, which is what we all fear about dying.

We must lose the fear of being out of control. Did you learn to swim when somebody just pushed you out in the water and said, "Now, just lie on your back and float." All of a sudden you were floating, not sinking. You just allowed it to happen. That's what we're asked to do on the Program — to give up the control and let it work for us.

One way to deal with our resentments and angers is to write about them. Writing about resentments and angers really is a lot like listing our fears. Sometimes in your Fourth Step inventory, you discover how angry and resentful and fearful you really are. But you may find it helpful to write an inventory specifically about your angers and resentments.

Divide a page down the middle. On one side, list what your angers are, and on the other side, list what you perceive as the causes, the reasons for your angers.

Pick a personal event. I am angry at the hotel clerk because he didn't save a room for me. I'm angry at my husband for forgetting to stop at the store. You may have several simultaneous angers at the same person; that's okay. If we can't find the reason behind the anger, that's all right, too. We may know it, but often cover it up. The cause behind the anger is not as important as acknowledging your feeling.

We begin to see that anger, like any other character defect, can be dealt with in this way. If we inventory angers, fears, guilts, and approach those defects with honesty and the willingness to let them go, they too will be taken away from us.

The promises of the Program are always achieved, not just with the food or alcohol, but with all aspects of our life. The important thing to see is that all these character defects — including anger — are barriers. They are invisible walls between our present selves and the new person we'd like to become. How can we be free to enjoy ourselves and the world about us when we see it distorted through barriers of anger, hate, and resentment?

If we look at our character defects not as wrongs, but as barriers, things that interfere, then we will know how to break down the barriers. Living the Program of recovery and then accepting God, as we understand him, will help us remove the barriers, so that our anger will not exist anymore.

The energy used to act out fear or anger can now be channeled into more productive and positive endeavors, which in their own ways will become just as exciting and certainly more fulfilling.

Fear and Depression

My compulsive overeating stunted my emotional growth and maturity and affected my physical well-being. However, once the compulsion to eat was removed, other problems started to take its place.

Food was easier to deal with. I could always look in the mirror and get upset about how fat I was or feel guilty about how much I ate. Coping with other more subtle problems and emotions is more difficult, since the consequences may not be so apparent.

I had many emotional problems which I had to discover and deal with. I found out that I had angers I never knew about. I also had fears that permeated my existence. I discovered that I had a problem relating to individuals. I finally "heard" my sponsor who had been telling me that for years. When you work so often with groups, and a lot of people seem to love you and you love them, especially in this Program, you can forget how to relate on a one-to-one basis.

The real crux of the matter is this: if you live the Twelve Steps in all your affairs, you will lose weight automatically. You will also lose a lot of other things in the process: anger, resentment, depression, hostility, etc. All these and your appetite will disappear. You won't even notice that they are gone. One day you will be standing out there and you will not be angry.

All those years I had layers of fat along with layers of one-level relationships and layers of money games. When I started the Program all these defects were being removed and what emerged was a very basic feeling — fear.

I have just as many fears, frustrations, anxieties, and compulsions as anybody, but I also have absolute faith that this Program will work for me and that there is a God out there. This God has nothing else to do but follow me around and take away my fear — also, my anxieties, my compulsions for food, the limits on my relationships, and any other problems I might have.

I want to be healed . . . even though I'm some-times comfortable being depressed, even though I often feel alive when I'm afraid or when I'm angry (especially when that anger is justified). For these reasons, I don't always want to give up my feelings. But in order to be healed I am willing to give up those feelings and to work this Program.

Fear and depression somehow work together. When you are afraid, do you ever have the sensation of freezing, almost like you are paralyzed? Freezing is a throwback to our earliest times. Humans' first defense against force was to stand still, just as most animals instinctively freeze in order not to be noticed, to blend in. One of the best ways I know to freeze is to get into a non-feeling state of depression.

I used to love to get depressed because depression was a method of escaping from life. When I was a little boy, it served two purposes: one was to protect me from the world out there; another was to attract attention. (Part of our craziness demands that we be noticed.)

I used to buzz my secretary and say, "Give me fifteen minutes. I want to be depressed." She would hold my calls and I would allow myself a beautiful state of depression. Depression was like an old girl friend. It was like going home to mother. I really felt comfortable in my old familiar feelings of depression.

I don't have those feelings anymore. I can't think of the last time I was depressed — I know it's been a long time. That doesn't mean that I'm not unhappy at times, but what I do about not being happy is to just allow it to happen, rather than actively creating and enjoying depression.

There is no rule which requires that everything must be terrific all the time. When I get a parking ticket, I'm not particularly happy about it. When someone gives me a check that bounces, I don't jump for joy. Yet I no longer react to these situations with depression.

Each of us has different fears, but some are basic to all of us — for example, the fear of dying. Or when someone close to us dies, often we are left with guilt about surviving or about not doing something to prevent the person's death.

Also, we have to live with fears of so-called failure, but I've come to the conclusion that my fear of failure is a fallacy. My real fear is of success, because when I am successful I am going to have to do things successful people do, like grow up.

I'm hardly ever afraid anymore. That doesn't mean I don't have respect for fearful things — I have respect for the Internal Revenue Service and speeding vehicles. I don't tangle with either, but I'm not afraid of anything or anybody anymore.

As a matter of fact, I've found out that I never was afraid of anything or anybody that existed at the moment. I was afraid of things that were long since gone or that hadn't happened yet. I was never really afraid of what was now. Furthermore I used my fears to feel bad about me, to prevent me from accomplishing anything. I don't do that now because I like myself. When you feel good about yourself, you can't be afraid.

We all have different fears and our deepest fears we often are totally unaware of. Fear prevents some of us from flying in airplanes or climbing a mountain or entering a crowded room. For all of us, fear can be — and usually is — very debilitating. Fear, which prevents us from functioning, becomes just another barrier we use to stop us from growing up.

I don't know what you can do about your fears, but I know that for me, it is most important that I recognize first that I *am* afraid.

As long as I can remember, I've had feelings of fear. When I was a little kid, I was afraid of big kids and I was afraid of my parents. I was afraid of being beaten. I was afraid of pain. I was afraid of letting my feelings show.

Now those little childhood fears have been translated into adult fears. I would feel silly if I went around saying that I'm afraid of the dark. That's not appropriate for an adult, even though it's still true for me. You see, I still have the same childhood fears, except I've translated them into adult terms. For example, instead of saying, "I'm afraid of the dark," an adult might say, "I'm afraid of being mugged" or "I'm afraid of being attacked" or "I'm afraid of being alone."

A fear that prevents me from functioning, that paralyzes me, interferes with my growth. Since I don't want to interfere with my growth anymore, I want to get rid of my fear. My fear is a character defect, but the Program says that there is nothing I can do about my character defect. When somebody I sponsor calls me up and says, "I've come up with this character defect, and I'm fearful my boyfriend will leave me. What can I do about it?" I say, "There's nothing at all that you can do about it." You see, the Sixth Step says that we must be entirely ready to have *God* remove all our character defects, and then the Seventh Step says, "Humbly asked Him to remove our shortcomings."

Fear is one of my character defects. So, I first have to recognize my fear and then I must become willing to get rid of it. I'm not willing to get rid of a lot of fears, because they have served me in good stead all my life. I have functioned all my life with my character defects. Now you take away a good, juicy character defect and I feel empty.

There is nothing as boring as to be unafraid. Just try it sometime. When everybody's around and they are all worried about dying and you're not worried, they think you're a little weird. You're not. You see, you're serving no purpose if you're wrapped up in a fear of your death — or someone else's — or, for that matter, in fear of abandonment by a friend, lover, or spouse.

When I made a list and recognized my fears, then I was willing to get rid of them. This willingness is sometimes hard to come by, since we are under pressure from those around us *not* to get rid of our fears.

When I was a kid, I remember that the person who upset me the most was the one who didn't give a damn. Did you ever meet the kind of kid who never cared whether or not you were his friend? This used to unnerve me since I wanted to be recognized as a friend. The ones who seemed to have the most friends were the ones who didn't seem to care.

Also, the ones who seem to have the most in life are the ones who don't worry about being afraid. When I'm afraid, the only way I can handle my fear is *not to handle it.*

We all say we don't want to be afraid any more, but if you really think about it, do you really want to get rid of your fears? Certainly we don't want to lose them all at one time. I mean if I were a fearless person, if I were perfect all of a sudden, what would I have to talk about with my family and friends. If someone says, "You know, the stock market's fallen," or "I'm out of a job," or "The kid just ran off with a dope fiend," and you say, "Yes, I know, and I'm not afraid." What would we talk about then? Our lives would be void of discussion.

Fear is a convenient focal point in life for most of us — especially for people who lose weight and put it back on. There is the fear of losing weight and all that this entails. What is life going to be like thin?

I first learned to recognize my fears by making a list. The second step was to check off the last, the least fearful, thing on my list, and to be willing to have God remove it. The third step was to allow God to remove it. After that I would go on to the next item of fear on the list.

In the long run, there's nothing we ourselves can do about our character defects. I, personally, don't have to cure me or you anymore. I don't have to make a large production anymore about how I'm going to lose weight, which was my most obvious character defect when I came to this Program.

What a wonderful unloading to allow a power to exist who can take care of all these burdens for me. Giving over that power to God has relieved me of the burden. I don't have to diet anymore; I have absolute faith that God's going to take care of that character defect. I don't have to worry about my fears any more. I have absolute faith that God will take care of them one by one. Of course, He may take care of one fear and one or two more come up. But that's okay. I can get up in the morning and be afraid, but I know that sooner or later in the day those fears will go away.

This can be a very difficult and illogical Program. It's illogical to be willing to let go of something that served me so well all my life, such as fear. It's illogical to trust what I can't see and have never believed in — that God has nothing else to do but take away my appetite and my fears. Yet that's what I'm asked to believe in, and I do. Gradually my fears (fortunately I am able to see them now) are being taken away one by one. That doesn't mean that the problems that seem to cause the fear are really solved. They're not. But the fear is removed.

I spent many moments of my life in fear that I felt I had to cover up. Although nothing has changed out there in the world, I now feel happy and joyful and able to get on with living.

When I was hurting, there was nothing that deadened the pain better than bingeing. That way I didn't have to look at my fears.

Invariably the drunk who does nothing but stop drinking is going to start drinking again. The addict who stops using dope is going to start using it again. And the compulsive overeater who does nothing but diet is going to start eating again.

Until you are hurting badly enough, the steps won't work for you. It may take a long time for you to reach this point, but that's okay too, because dieting together in a fellowship is better than dieting alone. I'd rather be with a bunch of friends who understand me — who, if I binge, would be there to support me and help me back.

If you are paralyzed, there is nothing you yourself can do. There is probably no human power that can relieve our fears — anymore than any human power can relieve our compulsive overeating. So why do you bother to try on your own? What a lifting of the load to know that you can be afraid and you don't have to do a thing about it!

The problem with this paradoxical idea is that it's the opposite of everything we've ever done in our lives. We've been told all our lives, "Stop that!" "Do this!" "Do that!" "Get on with it!" "Run here!" Yet this Program tells us there is nothing we can do except to *be willing to let God remove it from us.*

There is footwork to be done, but not on the specific problem of fear, depression, anger, or whatever. The footwork to be done is on the Program. If I am working these Twelve Steps, God will remove my fear. If I am working these Twelve Steps, God will remove *all* of my character defects. But I'm not going to be willing until the defects hurt enough.

The Program asks a great deal of trust and faith of us, especially when we have visual proof that every time we trusted, we got kicked. Every time I thought I trusted somebody, I always got a kick. Now, along comes a Program initiated by a bunch of drunks, and they tell me to trust again.

Most of us come to this Program to just test the water a little bit. "Okay, I'll try your Program, but if I don't lose ten pounds this week, the heck with you. I'll give you a chance, but if I don't feel this love and affection I've heard about immediately and lose my extra weight, well then, I'm going to go back to diets."

Every once in a while, I still lose a little faith and trust. Who am I to think that God has nothing better to do than take care of my office while I'm away, for instance. I have to believe He has nothing else to do. I used to have a terrible fear that a catastrophe was going to happen to my office if I wasn't there. So when

I felt that fear, I purposely did not call my secretary when I was away. See, that's just like eating as far as I'm concerned. That is giving in to the fear — being overpowered by it. God removed the fear from me. If I do call when I'm not fearful, of course, I discover that everything is fine.

The only magic I know is the miracle of this Program. The only way I know how to find the miracle of this Program is to work the steps. The Big Book says about fear: "This short word somehow touches about every aspect of our lives. It was an evil and corroding thread. The fabric of our existence was shot through with it. It set in motion trains of circumstances which brought us misfortune we felt we didn't deserve." But we ourselves started the ball rolling. The Big Book says to review our fears thoroughly, put them on paper, even if they had nothing to do with our resentments.

This is an inventory of fears. For those of you who are afraid to write inventories . . . DO IT ANYHOW! We ask ourselves why we have these fears. Self-reliance has failed us. Self-reliance was good as far as it went, but it didn't go far enough to solve the fear problem or any other. When self-reliance made us cocky, that made things worse.

We are now on the basis of trusting and relying upon an infinite God, rather than our finite selves. We are in the world to play the roles God assigns to us; we do as we believe He would have us do.

"We never apologize to anyone for depending upon our Creator. We can laugh at those who think spirituality is the way of weakness. Paradoxically it is the way of strength. The verdict of the ages is that faith means courage. All men of faith have courage. They trust their God. We never apologize for God. Instead we let Him demonstrate, through us, what He can do. We ask Him to remove our fear and direct our attention to what He would have us be. At once we commence to outgrow fear," says the Big Book (p. 68).

That last sentence doesn't say that God actually *removes* the fear. It says that we outgrow fear. Fear served a purpose for us. Unless we're willing to give up fear, it won't go away. It's that gap between our maturity and our emotions that creates the anxiety, and we use fear as a means of covering it up. What happens is that as we grow, emotional maturity grows and grows until the gap diminishes. Instead of pain being covered up, the pain ceases.

To me, fear is a terrible inconvenience. It wastes my time and I don't want to indulge in it. I have too many important things to do to waste my time being afraid. So I'm outgrowing fear on a daily basis.

Write an inventory about fear. Share with other people your fear experiences and how you have outgrown fear — if you have — and how you utilized the help of the Program to do so. Those of us who are still fighting fear can then grow by your experiences.

Sometimes we hear speakers who share and aren't even aware of what they are doing, of how they are helping us. Their experiences may sound minor, but sometimes they are crucial for the well-being of a person who is listening.

When you write an inventory, it is important to see how you can utilize it. The important thing is to hear those words, "allow God to remove it," so we can begin to outgrow fear. Fear doesn't serve a useful purpose anymore, any more than compulsive overeating does. So when you write inventories, then you can see your character defects in their many aspects and you will see your long time relationship with fear — the little fears and the big fears.

The littlest fear is often the biggest fear, and huge fears turn out to be nothings. Sometimes we use small fears to disguise our real ones, to hide from what we are really afraid of.

Once God removes fear from you, you will find that you have other matters to take care of. The purpose of an inventory is not only to point out your character defects and how you use them, but to allow you to see persons you have harmed with your character defects. You are aware that you have hurt yourself by your fears, but may be surprised at how many others your fears have hurt along the way.

Money

Money! I've known for a long time that I had a problem with money, but I thought it had to do with not earning enough. I was positive that somehow having more money would indicate a change in my life and everything else would fall into place — the same way I'd been so sure that being thin was all I needed to make me happy.

When I lost my extra weight, I had other problems to deal with. I told myself, "Well, when you're thin you have to be able to go into an expensive store and buy thin clothes." When I got thin, I said, "If only I were rich, too, I'd have everything I wanted in life." But even the fact that there was never enough money didn't stop me from going into expensive stores to shop. When I want something, I want it.

I would just as soon go without shoes as buy a pair of cheap shoes. I still will go without them until I can afford to buy the best. As with most compulsive overeaters, the child in me often gets its way. This is still a part of my insanity; I will buy what I want and refuse to settle for anything less.

I didn't want to play tennis with any old tennis racquet. I had to buy an expensive one. It didn't improve my game at all, but I felt better because I had a good racquet.

I began to look at my dealings with money. How crazy to get "dunning" letters when I had the money to pay the bills! But I sat with money in the bank to pay bills and I wouldn't let go of it. Also, if I were to pay right away, then the problem would be over. I didn't like things to be over.

Until I stopped doing this, I didn't realize how similar this problem was to my insanity about food or to any of my other character defects. Apparently I didn't *want* problems to be over. What would I do without the anxiety of unpaid bills? What would I do to fill that void? Anyone who chooses to put off abstaining from compulsive eating will understand what I mean.

I had the same anxious feeling when I would walk away from food or leave it on the plate; I felt as if the day were not complete somehow.

I would sabotage myself by accumulating bills, telling myself I would take care of them on Friday. Then on Friday, I would be busy and I'd say, "What's the difference if I put them in the mail today or not? They won't arrive until Monday or Tuesday anyway. So paying them on Monday is the same as paying them on Friday." Then when Monday came, I'd vow to take care of them that evening . . . or Tuesday . . . or Wednesday. I would rationalize so much that pretty soon, instead of eighty or a hundred dollars of unpaid bills, I would have piled up close to a thousand.

When I asked my secretary to make out the checks, I would try not to look at the bills. That way, I could make believe they were not there. "When you open the mail," I'd say, "just give me the letters."

She'd stand firm and say, "We'd better take care of the bills. You need a thousand dollars in the account."

"A thousand dollars! There were just a couple of bills there!"

"You let them accumulate for weeks," she would report.

Then, all of a sudden, I would have a lot of anxiety. What I had done was to set up the whole anxiety-producing situation.

You see, it hurts me to sign checks. The fact that I owed the money in the first place had nothing to do with my feelings.

I began to see that money in the bank had no value. It was just like the food I used to store in the refrigerator — I was glad to know it was there, so that I could look forward all day long to sitting in front of the television and eating my stock of favorite foods. The evening was empty for me if I couldn't eat.

I have found out since that there are plenty of other things to do to fill up my life. When I first came to this Program, I used to go to a lot of meetings. How could I sit at home and *not* watch television and eat. Instead, I might have to notice things around me or recognize my feelings or communicate. I might even have to use my brain to occupy my time. When I gave up eating in the evenings, it was sad — just as if someone took a book away when you reached the final chapter.

That's how I felt about relationships, too. When you start giving up inappropriate, crazy relationships, you miss the excitement. Going out with an ordinary person who is not going to destroy your life is not exciting.

I had the same feelings about money. When I gave up gathering debts, I would actually miss the anxiety — the excitement — of a stack of unpaid bills. Even when I began to see the light, I kept sabotaging myself. I treated myself like a baby, because I *was* a baby when it came to money matters. If I had two hundred dollars in my pocket, I felt rich.

I lost a sense of proportion about money. What was important was not what money could buy, but that it represented power to me. And if I had power, I was in control.

People use money in several ways. Some can't bring themselves to spend money, and some spend too much. I've been at both extremes.

As long as I played these money games, then I didn't have to deal with my fears, angers, and resentments. I could cover them up.

Now I have my secretary's signature validated to sign checks on my bank account, so that the bills are paid right away. I don't want to live anymore with all that anxiety about money.

Anyone who is used to carrying over until tomorrow the problem of money — or food or relationships or whatever — is very lonely when the problem is gone. We have such a hard time understanding that the real problem does not have to do with food or money or relationships. The real problem is that we don't want to grow up. If I choose to grow up, I may discover that being grown up is boring.

Have you noticed how children — little kids about eight or ten years old — almost never sit still? They are always doing, going, running. Even when they try to sit still, their feet are moving. Well, that's how I was inside all the time. There was a little kid in there who wasn't happy just to sit still and let life go around him. So when it came to money, I could not just pay a bill and be done with it. Sometimes I would let checks bounce even when I had the money to cover them because I couldn't bring myself to transfer the money.

How many of us, when we have a task or job to do, keep putting it off? This delay builds a level of anxiety in us. We then have to rush to do it. When we hurry, we usually mess it up — or we don't do it at all, so we're scolded or shouted at and we feel guilty.

I used to procrastinate. Then when a client would get impatient and leave me to go to another attorney, I would be rewarded by being righteously angry. "Why, look at all the work I did for that person!" The client (by now an ex-client) would say, "Good work, but a little late." Did you ever make dinner for company and forget to cook the vegetable? All through the meal preparation, you kept telling yourself to get the vegetable ready. Then you trot out your finest china and a beautiful dinner — and someone in your family says, "Where's the broccoli?" And you have to answer, "Uh, I forgot it."

Money itself is not the problem any more than food is the problem. But both provide us with some very convenient everyday situations that we use to make us feel bad about ourselves. We justify our behaviors, but basically, underneath it all, we know what we're doing.

Money games are insidious. A woman travels miles to save a nickel; then she justifies the trip by thinking, "What a good wife I am! I'm so thrifty!" A husband doles out money to his wife in bits and dribbles justifying his stinginess by saying she can't be trusted.

Probably we all could earn a good living if we wanted to. When I first went out and practiced law, I remember saying, "The week that I earn a hundred dollars, we are going to go out and celebrate." Then I earned a hundred dollars one week and had so many bills to pay that there was no money left for celebrating. Now that my ability to earn is limitless, I still limit it sometimes. We all put limitations on ourselves.

Playing around with money is deadly. Usually we don't see the results the way we do with food because we don't get fat over it . . . You can always say that the reason you don't pay bills is that you don't earn enough money. But when I was insane, there was not enough money in the world to satisfy my insanities. No matter how much money I made, I could always find a way to go broke.

If you deal with people's finances as I do, you see the games they play with money in order to create anxiety.

The Twelfth Step requires that we "practice these principles in all our affairs." I see successful weight-losers all the time who end up going back to food.

That's because they haven't cleaned up their acts with relationships, with money problems, or with work problems (which, of course, often involve money, too).

They are refusing to grow up. Why? Because when you grow up, you have to deal with down-to-earth problems, which is not very exciting.

It's time for all of us to grow up. And that even applies to newcomers to the Program. When I first came into the Program, almost everybody was a newcomer.

All we talked about for the first three or four years was what and when and how much we should eat. Gradually, more and more, we stopped talking about food, and all of a sudden we discovered that the Twelve Step Program was really a spiritual program. So we talked about God a lot. Now some of us have found out that we are not just supposed to talk about God; we are supposed to live a spiritual program.

Living a spiritual program means dealing every day, moment by moment, with the consciousness of God. That means that when you park next to a meter, you put a nickel (or whatever it requires) in it. That means making deposits in the bank on time and buying sensibly — not rewarding your insanities by going on a shopping spree. That means taking care of financial responsibilities without procrastinating.

The Program has grown — and hopefully we have grown too — to a point where we can handle these problems.

Three or six months from now, when you happen to be in a department store handing your charge card to a salesperson, you might stop and think. And you will say, "No, I'm going to pay cash for it instead." Or you might say, "You know what? I really can't afford that. I'm not going to buy it." I hope you will walk out of the store and feel good about it. You'll announce to yourself, "I'm not going to play money games anymore."

What is there to do with our lives, now that we have cleared up — or are in the process of clearing up — these character defects? We can find plenty to do. There is new excitement and joy in just keeping yourself company, so you never have to be lonely again.

You will always be lonely if you can't live with yourself. I don't care how many people are around you or how many accolades you earn, you can still be lonely. Or you can be alone and not be lonely at all. "Alone" and "lonely" are not synonymous.

I never feel alone; I feel the presence of God at all times, as well as the presence of others in this Program. After years of not liking myself, I can now enjoy just being with me.

There are always options in life. The alternative to compulsive overeating is not spending the rest of your life ruling out certain food items. The option is that you can eat some of those things once in a while, *but you don't have to.* You are not even going to want to.

The alternative to playing money games is not giving up forever all shopping in expensive stores. The option is that you can shop there, because you will probably be able to afford to — but, knowing that you can afford to, *you don't have to do it anymore.*

Now that I know I can pay for them, I don't have to buy expensive things anymore. I'm as comfortable in an inexpensive shirt and jeans as in a shirt with a fifty-dollar monogram and custom-tailored slacks. I still enjoy expensive shoes, but the feeling of needing them has gone.

If we want to work the Program, we have to work on relationships, money, appropriate dress, cleanliness, fears, angers, depressions — all these concerns — or we'll go back to eating.

This is no halfway program. You either do it or you don't do it. The hope is that you will stay with it long enough to have the "spiritual awakening" the steps talk about.

Just being thin is not the answer. When I came into the Program, my idols were the thin ones. Whatever they did, I did. They dieted, so I dieted.

When they started putting their weight back on after their diets, I was scared. I certainly didn't want to do that. Fortunately, I got so frightened that the thought of putting the weight back on was worse than the thought of having to work hard at this Program to find out what it was all about.

So I proceeded on my journey. I am still proceeding. Every time I think I see the journey's end, around the bend there's another valley or hill to cross. Every time I start cleaning up one mess in my life, I go around the corner and find a sign that directs me another fourteen miles down the road.

In talking to women about money, I find that a lot of women feel that money matters are out of their control because the husband traditionally runs the family finances. That's not womanly; that's childish. If your marriage is based on fear while you enable a situation of economic insecurity to continue, you are prostituting yourself like any call girl or street-walker. If you don't see your participation in this kind of insanity, then chances are good that you will mess up your life as you have before by seesawing up and down with weight gains and losses.

The Big Book says to approach this Program with rigorous honesty, with the very essence of truth. The biggest lie we compulsive overeaters live is to appear to be what we are not. To appear to be a woman when you are still a little girl is a lie.

Women, as well as men, must take responsibility for finances. That doesn't mean you have to take over the checkbook or the bill-paying. But you can ask, "How much do you earn?" or "What happens to our money?" You can say, "Before we buy a car, I want to discuss it too," or "I have certain needs I want to talk about with you."

If your husband tells you it's none of your business because he is the one who is earning the money, you can counter with:"Then you can cook the meals and clean the house."

God in His own way has removed the problem of money for me. The Twelve Step Program works with money problems. If we search in our hearts, we will see that these insanities about money occur in most of us. In sharing these problems, we may be doing a service to others so they can see they are not alone.

Many of us have made money our god, just as we have made food a god. But there is no room in this Program — or in our lives — for more than one God.

Relationships

When we talk about relationships, the first thing we compulsive overeaters or alcoholics do is to acknowledge that we are *sick* people. That's why we are banded together in this Program.

Ours is a threefold illness. First, we are physically sick — obviously, since most of us are fat. Second, we are emotionally sick. People who don't have emotional problems don't eat the way we eat and don't live the kind of lives we live. Most important of all, we are spiritually sick. There is a part of us that has lost faith in everything, and that's why we eat.

We recognize, too, at all times when we deal with our families, our employers, employees, or friends, that *we* are concerned with *our* sickness. They may be sick, too, but *we* are the ones we're trying to change.

I always thought that if I just had enough love from people, then I would be happy. But I have all the love I can handle in this Program now, and sometimes it is still not enough. I find myself looking for that one guy who doesn't like me. We simply have to stop looking for someone to hurt us or make us feel bad. I was asked to speak at one meeting after they voted twelve to one to invite me, and I wondered who that one was. Then I thought, "My God, the insanity of *that!!*" You could be the most loved person in the world, and you're going to hook in to the one person who doesn't like you! That is an insanity which most of us will recognize.

A person looking for a relationship usually gives me an example of Mr. Perfect or Miss Perfect — you know, looks like a movie star, a professional person with a million dollars, kind and considerate. But if I brought you that ideal person, you would say, "Well, he (or she) is nice, but he (or she) doesn't turn me on."

You know what turns you on? Your own insanity, your own sickness.

We acknowledge that we are sick when we come into this Program. We hope that as time goes on we will be restored to sanity. That is the goal of the Program. We accept the fact that we are sick — certainly in our eating habits, and probably in other aspects of our lives as well.

The Big Book says on page 151 that for most people drinking means conviviality, companionship . . . release from care and boredom, intimacy with friends and a feeling that life is good. The same might be said of normal eaters. For alcoholics or for compulsive overeaters this is not true. As we binged and made food all-important in our lives, we found little pleasure in eating — only feelings of failure, fear, bewilderment, and frustration resulting from our lack of control.

If we are willing to admit that we are crazy when it comes to food, what makes us think all of a sudden we're sane when it comes to relationships? Also, after a time, we begin to wonder about the sanity of other members of our families. We believe that if our spouses had a degree of sanity, they wouldn't have married us in the first place!

If we have children, we feel that we must have passed our insanity on to them. If we have parents, we are convinced they passed it on to us, even though we don't hold it against them anymore. When someone hires us, we wonder why they did. If we hire someone, we wonder how that person stays around a crazy employer. We wonder why our friends want to be with a crazy person. Why? Because all these others were attracted by something they saw in themselves.

What happens when we become sane is that those around us — if they really are crazy — have to become sane, too, or they are going to find somebody else to be crazy with. As you raise the level of your Program of life, everything rises to that level. If your spouse wants to stay at the former level, he or she is going to find someone else at that level to play the old games with.

Your marriage is never going to be the same after you come to this Program. As you grow, your marriage will grow. Sanity is contagious. If you give it an opportunity, then those around you will catch on. When you're kind and considerate, not angry anymore, pleasant to live with, when you are a loving person, not only to eveybody else out there but to your family, then those others will be loving, too, if they are willing. If not, they will find others to be unloving with.

As for blaming others for your sickness, I always tell people to look in the mirror and see if *you* would like to come home to *you*. If you are down on someone you are having a relationship with, just think of who it is *that person* is having a relationship with!

It is we compulsive ones who are overweight and cannot handle the problems of life. It is we who don't know how to eat a normal meal. We are the ones our families and friends have suffered with. Forget about who or what caused our illness. Nobody's causing it now.

Some of us are still blaming our parents for what we are. Even in my thirties, when I came into this Program, I was still blaming my parents for things that happened when I was a child. My parents were dead and I was still blaming them. I blamed anyone and anything except myself. And yet I was *solely* responsible.

Some of us blame our spouses for what we are. Haven't you heard someone say, "I wasn't like this when I married him. I was thin all my life until I married him. What was I supposed to do while he watched football games on television. He drove me to food!"

We have only ourselves to blame for our compulsions now. Yet we still go around pointing fingers at everybody else. "If you didn't do this, I wouldn't do that." Even though we know better, we still want others to be responsible for our problems . . . That sounds logical and I am terrific at logic!

Obviously, if I go home, my wife should understand that I evaluate her love for me by whether or not the refrigerator is full. If she loved me, she would fill the refrigerator. Now that's logical, isn't it?

If she really loved me, she would *know* I like a certain movie. She should be able to read my mind. If you have to tell a person your wants and opinions, then that person really must not love you. That's how "logically" I would handle relationships. That's how my insane mind worked.

In this Program, we have found out that our state of mind is conducive to getting fat. Our compulsions began a long time ago. If we hadn't turned out to be overeaters, we probably would have had some other kind of compulsion.

Our Program tells us that there is a way out for us. We have a way of recovering from this state of mind and this physical being. However, we do need support.

Even after we have discovered the value of the Program, support means a lot of meetings and a lot of time away from our families.

Haven't you heard comments like, "My mother used to eat all the time, so she had no time for me. Now she's stopped eating all the time and gotten thin. She's gone back to school at night and got herself a job. Now she's always going to meetings. And she gets calls at 8 a.m. when she should be getting the kids ready for school, and she's talking to some fat guy on the phone. At least she tells me he's fat. And she *still* doesn't have any time for me."

Members of the family think maybe they were better off when she was fat.

We want families to understand, too, that it's difficult for a person all of a sudden to have a thin body. It is hard to hear, "My, don't you look nice!" when we have felt ugly all our lives. Sometimes we don't know how to handle this kind of praise. We want our families to know that we are going through a difficult period. We want them to understand that for *us*, this Program is more important than life itself.

We need more than just understanding from our families. We want them to join us. We need more than a spouse saying, "Well, that's nice. My wife (or husband) has gone down from that size to this size. She (or he) is really happy about losing fifty pounds."

Like the alcoholic whose wife became a drinking buddy or who tolerated her husband's alcoholic behavior, many of our family members became eating buddies. Now they may resent eating alone if you are off at a meeting, or watching you eat special foods, or fail to realize that you don't enjoy cooking what you can't eat.

To our spouses we say: Please don't ask, after we have lost weight and kept it off, "Well, now you don't have to go to those meetings, do you?" Or, "By now you should be able to have a piece of cake once in a while." We know these remarks are well-meaning, even loving. But we also know that giving in could kill us. We're not interested in changing anyone else's eating habits. You can do and eat what you want, but since we have abused our bodies, allow us the privilege of doing what we have to do for us.

Support does not mean that you have to carry us along. Sometimes we need you to be at our sides. Sometimes we may need you to leave us alone.

But this we have to say straight out: Our marriages are important. So are our jobs, our parents, our children, our friends. But there is nothing more important to us than this way of life. That may sound self-righteous and selfish, but we know that without this Program, we will not have our families and friends.

Many of us have found that no matter what kind of a relationship we had — with our children, our parents, our spouses, our friends — it was no relationship because we were half-persons. We weren't whole human beings. But now we want to change. We want to grow up.

In my relationships I'm now open to people. They no longer have to worry about approaching me. I am not going to hurt them or lie to them. I know that everything I do to hurt another person comes back to me tenfold. I am going to do nothing that will hurt *me.* We are so selfish about being thin that we are honest in order not to get fat. Honesty is difficult for us, because we have lied to ourselves for so many years.

We do not ask forgiveness, but indulgence, patience, love, and support. When we make our amends, we do it for us. If our apologies are accepted, that's great, but not necessary. We are still selfish to that extent.

We who are on the Program have just one goal in life: to serve other people and God. Now that may sound very high and mighty. It may even sound ridiculous. But do not mistake our service for weakness. See it for what it is — incredible strength. Because we rely on God, do not think that makes us unreliable people. We can be relied upon for *anything* because we have something we never had before — the power of a God within us. Because we have trust in a Higher Power, we don't have to rely upon anyone else for strength, hope or feelings. Our Higher Power gives us the ability to be thin anytime we want. He gives us joy and happiness beyond anything that we have ever known in our lives.

Sometimes members of our families think they have failed. They say, "We should be able to give you what some book written by a bunch of drunks seems to give you. It's not your fault that you're fat; it's ours." To our families and close friends we say: In order for you to understand our new way of life, there are programs for families of compulsive overeaters that teach you how the steps can be applied in your lives, too. Even if you say, " *I* don't have a problem," *we* are a problem to you. You can learn how to deal with us. We recommend such a program to you, but your going there is strictly your choice.

In the Big Book, Chapter Eight ("To The Wives"), Chapter Nine ("To the Family Afterwards"), and Chapter Ten ("To the Employer") all are about the alcoholic's — or the compulsive overeater's — relationships with other people. These are chapters that other people are supposed to read in order to understand the compulsive person. When we work on these chapters in our Program, we often ask spouses, boyfriends, girlfriends, parents, children, employees, employers — all those we are relating to on a continuing basis — to "relationships meetings."

They may protest and say, " *I* could put down a sandwich" or "*I* don't have to drink" or "*I* don't gamble." That may be true for them. But we know that we *can't* and we *do*. And we need their understanding. We need them to understand the nature of our compulsion.

There is no way in the world we can stop our compulsive behaviors by the threat of divorce or the loss of children or parents — or even death. We *can* stop eating compulsively, but we *can't stop by ourselves*. We can only stop by faith and trust in God.

We get that faith and trust through this Program. The Program is based upon a simple principle: We get what we give. The more we give to others, the more we get back. We have only one path left open to us — we have blocked off all others. That is to do service to other people and God.

You, our families, are "other people." You are entitled to our service. We don't always like serving husbands who we feel have given us reasons to eat, or wives who have driven us from our homes, or children who remind us of the way we were, or parents who we may believe made us what we are. Still, we do it.

Our Program begins first in the home. If we can't work it in the home, if we believe that we can work it only at meetings or on the telephone, we are making a mistake.

Overeaters Anonymous is not a club of dieters. It is a fellowship of sufferers who don't want to suffer anymore. We have to work our Program in *all* our affairs — at work, at play, with our families and friends. We cannot work this Program selectively — dealing only with the problem of weight.

Being of service to those around us does not mean being their slaves. We are through being people-pleasers. We serve them not because they demand it, or even request it, but because this is the only path left for us. We will have peace of mind in exact proportion to the peace of mind we bring into the lives of others.

We ask our families and friends to be understanding, considerate, and supportive as we are changing, day by day. We want them to understand that this is a spiritual Program. It does not teach people how to eat. It offers a methodology whereby they can recover from being the kinds of people they once were. We believe that recovery comes not through any other human, but from the High Power that we call God.

When I came into the Program, they talked about God, and I didn't want to hear. I usually don't want to hear about things that hurt. The reason I came to know and believe in God is because my life has become a miracle.

When I found out that there is a God of hope and trust, and that if I had hope and trust in that God, He would take away my appetite, that is exactly what happened. My relationships cleared up with my family and friends. I became a different friend because I became a different person. For the first time, I became a human being. I have feelings now. I'm afraid, but in a different way. Now I can cry. Before, I didn't know how to cry. I can love. I didn't know how to love before. I hurt, whereas once I was impervious to hurt, because I had denied my own feelings.

We shouldn't deny our feelings; we shouldn't deny other people their feelings either. When you say to someone, "Don't cry," you invalidate that person's feelings. Don't deny others their right to feel.

Don't be a people-pleaser. Be willing to risk friendships. Above all, be honest with others, as well as with yourself. Have relationships with people not out of fear or need, but out of choice. Learn the difference between your need and your pleasure.

The most important thing I've learned about feelings is not to label them as good or bad. Some are very uncomfortable, even so-called good feelings.

For instance, we all say that we want to be loved, and yet one of the most uncomfortable feelings I used to experience — and to a certain extent still do — was when somebody wanted to hug me. Try this sometime: put your hands at your side and let somebody hug you. You might feel an overpowering smothering of somebody's affection for you, even though that is supposed to be a good feeling. Still, in spite of the discomfort, by allowing ourselves to be loved, we are going sane. Similarly, we can look and say, "I can see my body now, and it's not as fat as it used to be. I can literally see what I am doing: I am going sane."

When we are angry because a husband or wife did this or that, we ask God each day what we can do for that person. So the next time a family member is short-tempered or impatient with you, ask "What can I do for you?" And mean it when you say it. That person may look shocked and tell you that you are *really* crazy. Then you can say positively, "No, I am going sane."

You see, your life depends upon doing for that person — and for others. Not doing it his way or her way, but God's way. What you are offering in your relationship is a better person — you. That is what you can do — and be — for God, for others, and for yourself.

So to our families and our friends: As we become more and more sane, we begin to want better relationships. Don't fight us; join us. Together we can trudge that happy road of destiny. And God will bless you and keep you, too.

Recovery

I led a retreat once in a beautiful mountain area. After it was over and we were driving down the mountain, I sensed that the "high" — that good, alive feeling that comes from fellowship and sharing this Program — was beginning to leave me. I felt as if I wanted to eat something — a feeling that I had not had for a long time.

When I was feeling good, I didn't need to eat. But as I was losing that "high," I seemed to want a reward. I could maintain that good feeling if I thought about food and got excited about it.

This episode left me with an understanding that, as a compulsive person, I have been vacillating all my life between extremes of feeling very high or very low. Unless I was at one end or another of the emotional spectrum, I didn't feel alive.

Being on middle ground emotionally was not very exciting for me, so I never stayed on an even keel for long. As a kid, I often manipulated those around me by being depressed. Even in my relationships, I was always quick to categorize people according to the way I reacted to them. When I met someone, if I did not feel that special excitement, positive or negative, then that person was not worthy of my time. If I had no feeling at all, I just didn't bother with that person.

Now, being on emotional middle ground has relieved me of an incredible burden. I have let go of anxiety-producing extremes. I don't have to feel low. I don't have to feel high. I don't have to be the best. I thought if I couldn't be the best, I had to be the worst! If I wasn't fat, I had to be skinny. If I wasn't bingeing, I had to be starving. I remember when I first lost my weight, I had a euphoric high — we call it the honeymoon. I came off that with a jolt. Fortunately, I didn't put my weight back on. Now I've found a balance between extremes. How this balance came about I don't know. As the Program promises, it came so automatically I never noticed it happening.

I used to have a habit of being late. I would be in a state of anxiety because I had to be in two places at the same time. I'd have to figure out a series of lies to tell in order to excuse my tardiness. Now, I will look at my calendar ahead of time and realize I am supposed to be in two different places at nine o'clock so I'd better call a day ahead and change one of the appointments.

I was sure that if I messed up my schedule, someone might be upset, a client might be angry, my day would be ruined. I now acknowledge that I may be late sometimes and my client may be angry, that terrible consequences might happen — or they might not. When I accepted this, the anxiety left me.

"Letting go" is an art which involves more than simply letting things happen, more than just saying, "Now I'm going to let this problem alone." It is a willingness to *allow* it to happen. Let's say you are anxious because you predict that your wife or husband is going to yell at you and you won't be able to handle the situation. You build up a real case of anxiety. The point is that if you just accept the fact that it *may* happen, that, yes, your spouse *may* yell and scream and upset you, you will survive. You will get through the day one way or another.

All my life, I set myself up to be beaten down or I did a pretty good job beating myself if nobody else did. I created all the monsters in my life and lived with them. Where I allowed those monsters to leave me and gave myself the freedom to be imperfect, they disappeared. The process that led me to freedom is contained in the Twelve Steps. We have to go ahead and take the steps, these Twelve Steps, as well as other practical steps in our lives.

The act of "turning our lives over" is crucial to us, but it's difficult to release the future. We live so much in anticipation of what may happen, or in guilt or resentment about what did happen, that *now* never exists for us. We're always reliving the past or trying to control the future. Yet we can't really know what's going to happen tomorrow. Even if an event happened predictably a thousand times, it may not happen a thousand and one times. The pattern can end.

Things I never thought I was capable of doing, I have done. Changes I've made in my life are spectacular. If I can make these changes, anybody can do it.

The Big Book talks of examining our lives with "rigorous honesty," of seeking God with "complete abandon." You have to say to yourself, "Am I willing to give up, now and forever, compulsive eating? Am I willing to give up all those foods that have made me fat all my life? Am I willing to give up the habits, the addictive habits that plagued me all my life? Am I willing to allow God to take care of this problem, to have absolute trust that He can and will?" That's the "complete abandon" talked about. Am I willing for me to be imperfect? Am I willing for others to be what they are (since they are going to be the way they are anyway)?

You make a problem out of relationships when you make believe others are going to change — that all of a sudden, for instance, your parents are going to be the wonderful parents Andy Hardy seemed to have. They may sometimes be that wonderful, sometimes not. Your spouse probably is not going to change either. The children are going to be just as troublesome as they always have been. Your work is going to be as unsatisfying as it always has been — maybe even worse.

The difference is that you now have a plan. You have hope. We all do. After an airplane crashed in California, another pilot wrote a newspaper article in which he said that at least the passengers didn't know for certain they were going to die. Even though the passengers of a plane in trouble may scream in fear, they still have a glimmer of hope that they will survive.

This man wrote that the crew knew that they were going to die and thus were denied what the passengers had — hope. How terrible it was for the crew in those brief moments before the crash, as they worked furiously to keep the plane going, in full knowledge that they were going to die in seconds. Their lives were over. What this pilot was writing about was hope.

For me, life was such an ordeal that I thought there was no hope. My only hope was that one day it would end, that I would die and be relieved of my pain, of all the suffering and fighting.

Thank God, now I have hope because I have the tools of this Program, the Twelve Steps. No matter what I do, no matter how bleak life may appear, no matter how terrible the facts of any given situation may be, I have hope. If I'm willing to put enough faith in God, He will relieve me of my anxiety and bring me serenity.

Now I know exactly how to find peace of mind, even though sometimes I don't do it and still experience the old anxiety. Nothing has changed "out there." Maybe the plane will still crash, but I can have peace of mind and serenity. I feel safe and protected with God's arms around me.

If I deny hope for myself, I'm just like the crew in that cabin, headed for death. It is reassuring to believe — not just anticipate — that everything is going to work out. Catastrophes can be occurring around me, but I know I am going to be okay. What a serene feeling that is!

My serenity comes from working the steps in all situations. I am through having to please anybody. I'm able to say no when it's appropriate. I'm able to say yes without being afraid to. The fact that I'm able to live my life without those terrible fears gives me hope.

I've worked through all the anxieties of anticipation now and I am raw underneath. My feelings, my real feelings, now can come out.

Now I have no real fear of things to come. I have happiness. I have love. And I'm willing to allow any feelings to come in to me.

As I began to change and move on in my life, people around me worried about what was happening to me. "You're going through a depressing period. You're not the kind of person you used to be. What happened?"

I answered, "I don't know. I really don't know."

Sometimes I would just sit down and cry. I didn't understand why I was sad. Then I found out: I was sad because I was letting go of that little child who had lived inside of me all these years — the one who felt the pain of those early beatings, who felt the anxiety of being labeled a "crazy child," who felt the depression of avoiding life. That child who had been kicking inside of me all my life now was gone.

The sadness came from saying good-bye. I've had to complete that boy's existence and then let him go. This was not a deliberate or even a conscious act. But suddenly he was gone, where he belongs, into my past.

Nobody reminds me of my childhood anymore. I no longer view people I meet as reflections of my past, so that I deal with them in that context. I have completed that unhappy child's existence and allowed myself to pass through my teenage years and become what I am — an adult man. It was hard to let go of that child. But after many years on this Program, it happened automatically.

I have finished being a fat person. For a time, I was a fat person in a thin body. Now that's over. I haven't been fat for years, nor do I think as a fat person.

Also, I have completed the relationship with my parents, who both are dead now. I have let go. All that is left of the past are memories — some nice and some terrible. But I'm not a reflection of them anymore. I had to let go of the past and let it die, along with the Bill that used to exist, who does not exist anymore, even in fantasy. I cried over it.

It's like letting go of a drowning person, especially when that person wants to die. I wanted that child to go, but I kept pulling him back and recreating the whole unhappy situation. As an eight-year-old child inside a man's body, I recreated on a daily basis that child. Each day my life was dedicated to reviving that child, so, naturally, I reacted like a child who is pretending to be an adult by wearing grown-up clothes. I was performing, playing adult.

When I became a lawyer, I wore lawyer's clothes and acted like a lawyer. I mimicked. When I was a father, I mimicked. I could never get over the fact that I was a father. I was always one of the kids. I used to love to play on the floor with them. I felt like a kid with my wives, both of them. I created a situation whereby they took over the role of parent in our family, because I would not.

They would become angry, because I refused to fill the role of parent. Then I would get angry at them.

When they pushed me far enough, the angry child would emerge. All that is over, and it happened automatically.

Only rebellious children eat compulsively. Adults do not. That's why it's now impossible for me to continue to eat compulsively, because I'm no longer a rebellious child who is getting even with the world. Now I wake up each morning with a sense of rebirth.

Now I don't owe anybody. I don't even owe the past. I just owe to myself to live each day as God intended. All these changes came about through the hope that is embodied in the steps.

For a while, until the transition I mentioned took place, I kept filling my emptiness with other compulsions, because a child or a rebellious adolescent is compulsive.

During the time I spent vacillating between hope and lack of hope, my appetite came back. When I had hope, my appetite was removed. Every once in a while, I still forget about the steps and the Big Book. I forget about what my life is for and I become self-willed, self-centered. Sometimes I think I'm God, and there's not room for two of us around. And then my Higher Power catches me by saying, "Any time you want to take over, go ahead, You know you can run your life and everyone else's, too, if you want to. I have other things to do." But that happens to me less and less.

Sometimes, I want to pinch myself to see if I'm still alive. It's such a great feeling to go through life, and *just go through it.*

I was afraid I would lose the joy of living when I lost the hell of living. But the joy of living is always out there. True, I do not feel those highs, become so ecstatic anymore. Smoking marijuana, when I did it, would be accompanied by flushes, giggles, and ecstasy. But I was willing to give up ecstasy for happiness. When you have unnatural highs, you also have the extreme lows of those feelings of worthlessness, hopelessness, emptiness, anger turned inward.

My life was hopeless; it was out of control. What I was trying to do was to control it. I couldn't understand that once I really let my life go out of control, really let go, it would follow its own natural path. If you try to guide a little canoe in a roaring stream, you'll find that, if you let it go, it will go downstream anyhow.

My whole life was spent going down one-way streets in the wrong direction, trying to change the street signs. I thought I was right and everybody else was wrong. That's why I found the steps so difficult for me in the beginning. I had great doubts, which I felt must be overruled and overcome through the examples of the people on the Program. If I could see people take this Program and change their lives, then I would know whether I was right or wrong.

I would know if I was once again going against the stream or trying to change the street signs, heading in the wrong direction while everybody else was going right. Fortunately, I see more and more people willing to have hope and faith and trust in this Program, willing to turn their lives with complete abandon over to God.

That doesn't mean that we walk around with a "holier than thou" attitude. That doesn't mean that I'm perfect; sometimes I mess up my life by doing things that are wrong, sometimes even childish. I still beat myself over the head once in a while, but it happens less and less.

Recovery means liking yourself. One night we must have had a thousand people at the meeting I led. When it ended about 2:30 a.m., I had never been so high in my life from all that attention. Then I got on a plane to go home and . . . down went the high. Before I got off the plane, it was gone. I realized then that the ultimate stroke is the one you give yourself. The high that comes from the thousands out there, being attentive and loving, does not last very long. If you give yourself love, then you don't depend on everybody else's love. If you don't give yourself love, then you can soak up all the love in the world, and it's not going to last. You are the ultimate decision-maker as to what your life can hold through your willingness to have faith, hope and trust.

The steps aren't easy. They ask us almost to be saints. Obviously, none of us will attain spiritual perfection. But the road there is wonderful. I once read a comparison between the yellow brick road and drunkenness. I changed it to apply to compulsive eaters. Dorothy was looking for the Wizard of Oz to get her where she wanted to go. When she finally found him, he turned out to be no wizard at all, but a fake. Yet he pointed out that the Cowardly Lion had *always* had courage, that the Tin Man *always* had had a heart, and the Scarecrow a brain. He was able to show them that they already really had what they said they wanted.

Dorothy, he said, could always find her way home by herself, that the path was always there. All she had to do was want it enough. When she wanted it enough, she went home to Kansas. That's the way it is for us. The path is always there.

Bill W. and those recovering alcoholics put in words what they were given — a way that was there long before.

When people start working the steps, they are thin, no matter how much they weigh. It is only a matter of time until they take the weight off.

A story in the Big Book, "Physician Heal Thyself," is about a doctor who found AA and became very active in it. He realized that he had become a terrific sponsor in AA but he still didn't know how to work his Program with his family. He forgot to have fun with his family. So he went home to his wife and said he was willing to do what she wanted for the rest of his life — in fact, it would make him very happy. He went on to say that he noticed that she was the one who did the dishes all the time. So he vowed to do the dishes. He now does the damned dishes every night — but he's doing them.

All of you who have husbands and wives at home should realize that they don't know what's happening at a meeting, no matter how much you tell them. They may be scared or angry. They may not like the changes they see in you, especially those changes which happen without their help. Go to them and say, "I had a terrific time at the meeting. Now I'd like to do something for you. What can I do for you?"

That's really how our Program works . . . by doing something for somebody else. We are human beings created in God's image. We set about through different means to cover ourselves with imperfection. We want to be free of the bondage, of the prisons that we have built around ourselves. Honesty and truth and doing for others will make us free. We really could have found freedom with just one phrase from the Bible: Love thy neighbor as thyself. We could have found it in the age-old cry of religions: God is one. But we did not. We need these Twelve Steps.

Live the Program in your daily life. To the degree that you bring peace of mind to others, you will have peace of mind yourself. To the degree that you present an opportunity for abstinence from compulsions to others, those compulsions will be removed from you. You have an obligation to carry the message now. Scary? Certainly it is, because if we had had feelings of self-worth in the beginning, we wouldn't be here now.

Now we're being asked to have a lot of self-worth, understanding, and determination. As you go out and be free, allow others to be free, too. Mommy and Daddy are not causing your behavior anymore. Finish being a child. Finish being fat. Once you finish being a fat person inside the weight comes off outside. Finish being crazy and become sane. The way you do it is through the Twelve Steps. The way you do it is through God and helping others.

Thin Is Not Well

Many people, including myself, came to this Twelve Step Program with conditions. I was going to give it a try on the condition that I lost weight. I had to have some indication that I would become thin.

Some come to the Twelve Step Program when they believe that they have "hit bottom." They have lost everything. The compulsive person turns to this Program — whether you call it AA, OA, Emotions Anonymous (EA), Narcotics Anonymous (NA), Gamblers Anonymous (GA), or whatever — often out of a job and ready for a divorce, hitting bottom, as they say. That wasn't true for me. I had hit "rock top." I was respected in my profession, I was married, I had a nice family, a beautiful home, a good practice, a big car, all the outward indices of happiness. I had everything, but nothing mattered.

My whole life had been spent searching for the key to happiness and I knew for sure the "if only" something else happened would I be happy. My happiness was entirely determined by outside events.

I call this Program the end to my "if only" way of living. I used to think "if only" I were thin, or "if only" I were married, or "if only" I *weren't* married, or "if only" I were rich, or "if only" I could be like . . . or "if only" I had . . . , or "if only" I lived in . . . But all the time I was thinkng about my "if only's," I chose to be fat. You see I thought those "if only's" were all that stood between me and happiness. But when I was married, I gained more. And when I won an important case, I got fatter than ever. I moved into my new house and got even fatter!

I tried food for happiness, I tried drugs, money, and buying things compulsively. I believed the story told to me that I was somehow defective and that I lacked what it took to live right. I acted out my "defectiveness" and finally concluded that I was not happy because I was fat. I actually thought I had come upon the secret of my unhappiness. "If only" I lost weight, everything would change. However, the truth was just the opposite: I wasn't unhappy because I was fat — I was fat because I was unhappy.

The biggest revelation I have had in this Program is that nothing has changed out there. I got thin and the world didn't change for me, nor will it ever change. I work my Program and that's what makes the difference. I no longer have to change the world or other people. There are no more "if only's."

I must be the one to move on, to admit I am not perfect. Sure, I still get depressed. I will continue to have bad days, but that's okay. You see, there is no perfection except for God. God is perfect and this is His Program and this Program works perfectly. The fact that a perfect God exists in the midst of suffering and chaos lets me know that He accepts imperfection in all nature, including mankind. We are whole already because He is within us. Imperfection seems to be part of His plan to let us know He is here with us. Fat is not wrong and thin is not right. THINNESS WILL NOT MAKE YOU WELL, BUT WELLNESS WILL MAKE YOU THIN.

If you are really honest with yourself, you simply cannot work these steps and go on abusing others, or abusing your body with too much food. If you are committed to this Program, you cannot lie, cheat, steal, take dope, or drink too much. It's inappropriate, even impossible, to overeat and love yourself if you are working this Program.

You are the only one who really cares if you lose weight. If you lost one hundred pounds by tomorrow, you would not be loved any more or any less. In my grandiosity, I used to think the whole world noticed whether I was fat or not and was talking about it. But I was the one who couldn't buckle my belt or button my buttons. If I didn't attain some goal or other it was *because* I was fat. I really believed that my unhappiness was because I was fat. It took me a long time to understand that I was fat because I was unhappy.

If you *do* decide to work this Program, however, you are going to have a phenomenal life and you will never have to worry about your weight again. Food will become a matter of fact, a routine. ("Oh, yes, I have to eat lunch now.") If you put on a few pounds, you won't want to eat. You will just cut down your eating until the extra weight is gone again, with no diet, no hassle, no anxiety. You will not make food a problem the way you did. You will no longer be thinking constantly about menus and when and where you are going to eat next.

"Compulsive" means crazy, and I was crazy when it came to food. I was never going to get on with my life as long as I continued to make food a problem for myself.

We will never be able to deal with food logically and no amount of re-education will change this fact. But I can stop the abuse of a substance — food — and thus stop abusing myself. From the Big Book, we understand that our disease can be arrested to such a point that we can call ourselves recovered. We can say on a daily basis, "I am a recovered compulsive overeater." We can walk away from food free and unshackled.

However, in order to be free and happy, we must take those steps to turn our lives over to God. But we resist, because we don't want to let go of our control. We are caught up in a super-control pattern of fear and rigidity and emotionalism — even when it comes to food. We are busy measuring food and deciding about food. Shall I eat this or that — or not eat at all? By comparison, being sane is not really very exciting or dramatic. In fact, it's rather boring not to care about food and regard a meal as just a meal, just sustenance to keep us alive. But if we are ever going to find real happiness, we have to discover a way to unwrap ourselves from our food compulsions.

We have to *not care* about food, to turn that little dial in our minds to "don't care about food," and our lives will start working for us. This has nothing to do with fat or thin labels, or diets.

The Big Book says our compulsion will be relieved, so we keep waiting to feel like not eating compulsively, for the desire to eat to be taken away. It took me three entire years to understand that I am the one who has to make my life work for me, to let my compulsions go. Instead of blaming *God* for not *taking* my desires away, I have finally come to understand that working the Program is the process which allows *me* to *let* my insanity go.

Being sane may not be the most immediately attractive way to go about finding happiness, but being crazy doesn't work either. Inappropriate behavior messes you up every time. Any time I get angry or depressed when there is nothing to get angry or depressed about, or any time I eat compulsively, it is an inappropriate action. It is totally inappropriate for a thirty-year-old housewife to eat a series of candy bars or ice cream cones or three desserts like a ten-year-old child. We adults with children's emotions are insatiable; there is never enough!

We need to accept ourselves and our disease — compulsive overeating. If you are fat and compulsively overeating, you are going through life fighting what *is,* even though you may not like the idea that you have an irreversible disease.

Through this Program, I have been cured of the obsession of having to take that first compulsive bite. The physical fact of my compulsion is still there, but it only becomes a problem when I act on it. It is not the piece of candy that makes me fat, but my unwillingness to be what I am. If I eat that first piece of candy, I have said to myself at that moment, "I am a normal person." But I am not a normal person and that is a physical fact. I am myself — right or wrong, good or bad, tall or short, blue-eyed or green-eyed, compulsive in my eating habits or not. I don't have to *like* being myself. But I have to accept being what I am — a compulsive overeater. That's what Step One is all about.

Accept what you are, but be careful of using the label "compulsive overeater" to explain and rationalize crazy behavior. That can become another game we play to justify how we act. Don't buy into justifying your anger or your greed, for instance, because justification will work against you.

Don't wait for God to *make* you feel like working this Program. Go ahead and work it anyway, even if it seems uncomfortable. The uncomfortable way, for me, usually is God's way and the way of ultimate happiness. An alcoholic has to find a way to live without drinking, and we have to find a way to live without eating excess food. The answer for all of us compulsive types is the Twelve Step Program.

I don't have to be compulsive anymore if I use these steps and follow directions. When I started taking flying lessons, the instructor explained the laws of aerodynamics. When you want to go up, you point the nose of the plane down, and when you want to go down, you point the nose up. I thought I trusted that instructor. When I did my solo, and along came this mountain in front of me, I simply had to risk that what he had told me to do was right.

Now I find happiness just hearing about a newcomer to the Program throwing away the scale. I find happiness watching a flower bloom little by little. I used to hurl things at the birds outside my bedroom window — they were too noisy for me. Now I listen to their music. I can find greater happiness at a Program meeting than at any feast or drinking party I ever knew!

Can you imagine life without fear? The name of this Program should be Fear Anonymous. So many of us are unwilling to give up food or fear because we don't know what else is out there for us. But life is fantastic if we can just risk letting go of our fears and our food and anything else that is keeping us from living and growing.

I came into this Program in December, 1970, the only man at the meeting. I came to lose weight because I had tried everything else, including diet clubs, doctors with shots, and every diet in the world. They were all successful. I had been strong enough to discipline myself to give up dope and find a job, but *I could NOT keep my weight down.* Every time I went on one of those diets and lost weight, I would *always* gain it back.

As I began coming to meetings, I was armed with all my diplomas and degrees to prove how smart I was. I thought I knew all the answers, but I was seventy-five pounds overweight, and my life wasn't working for me. Were these women going to tell me the secret of happiness? I thought they were all crazy with all that hugging and clapping.

But I stayed to find out that there was a Power, and it wasn't just the group. I also found out that I had been the great god-believer of all time. I had more gods than there were hairs on my head. I certainly had made food my god — along with my children, my parents, the weather, and the guy who took my parking place. Anything that is greater than you are, that you give power to, that controls you, is your god.

I have this motto now: "Yield the right of way." If you want my parking place, take it. If you want to get in front of me in line, go ahead and do it. I no longer belong to the debating society about who comes first. I don't care if you want to win — your motives have nothing to do with me, because I don't have to lose. If I let you get in front of me, you are not taking advantage of me, because I am allowing it to happen. I am in charge, and I'm a winner. It is important for me not to lose, because I always lost in the past, both in reality and in my head. So now I yield the right of way. If they want to be right or first, that's fine. I have found that there is nothing as frustrating to people who have to win all the time than someone who lets them win!

One day I looked in the mirror and said, "In the Bible it says we were created in the image of God. If God is within me, then who am I to deny myself. That is what I have been doing all my life, denying that I was a creature made in God's image with His capacity to love. The capacity for happiness was within me all the time."

For a long time after I lost the extra weight, I was simply coping. I was not going to risk going back to being fat, but I still thought of food as my comfort. I was tortured constantly, fighting food, even though I was thin. But just coping was not much better than compulsively overeating. We are inclined to make up a bunch of rules and goals, and soon we — as well as those we sponsor — end up gaining weight because our obsession with eating has been transformed into an obsession with *not* eating. Much of the time we used to spend eating and thinking about food is now spent thinking about how *not* to eat.

Because I wanted to control it, life for me used to be divided into rights and wrongs, mostly wrongs. It was wrong for rain to fall because I didn't want it to rain. It was wrong for food to make me fat when I wanted to be able to eat like other people. I was always right, and the rules of life were wrong. Now I don't always have to like what happens, but I have learned that reacting appropriately will give me ultimate happiness. Accept the rain. Accept what is, and don't judge it as right or wrong.

We do not have to be guided, as we always have been in the past, by any long-standing concept of ourselves as we used to be. This Program and these steps help free you from your past so you can live *today*. You no longer have to buy into other people's opinions of you, their criticisms or their non-accepting attitudes.

Don't live in your past. The messages we have plugged into from our past are no longer valid for us. For instance, a growling stomach doesn't mean that I have to eat. I named a growling stomach "hunger" a long time ago. But to tell myself I have to eat because my stomach is growling is a lie. I lie to myself to give myself an excuse to act inappropriately.

Learn to live with discomfort. Are you saying you don't want to give up food because you don't want to be uncomfortable? Then are you saying you would rather have the discomfort of fat than the discomfort of not having food? What stops my hunger? Letting it go stops it. What stops my anger or self-pity? Letting it go stops it. If you will really let these things alone, they will disappear. If you will give up food as a problem in your life, it will cease to *be* a problem.

Are you into depression? Give it up right now. Are you into self-pity? Give it up right now. We use fat as a barrier to living and loving life. Anger, depression, fear — we go out of our way to enjoy these feelings.

I believe that this Program deals with one important choice: to be sane or insane. I believe my insanity is the problem, not compulsive overeating. The Second Step says, "Came to believe that a Power greater than ourselves could restore us to sanity." That, to me, is what the Twelve Step Program is about — not about losing weight, not about being sober, not about being free of addicting drugs.

I used to live by the idea that "everybody else does it, so why can't I?" But I did *everything* everybody else did — everything that was self-destructive — all at once.

Whatever the circumstances or experiences of our lives — whether they are as grave as the death of a family member or as seemingly trivial as a spouse's refusal to pay a bill — we come to the Program because our reactions to these circumstances are the same: we overeat. We really can't compare the painful circumstances of our lives, but we can realize that our degree of unhappiness is the same. My pain is the same as your pain because my reaction is the same as your reaction. *None of us would be here in this Program if there were not some amount of emotional disturbance in our lives.*

It is not the "fat" that brought us here — but the insanity of our compulsiveness. The only difference between our insanity and the craziness of people who are locked away is in how much time we spend being insane and how anti-social our behavior is. The fact that we seclude ourselves or are angry at ourselves or indulge in isolated depression does not usually make us prospects for mental institutions. We are not arrested for devouring three desserts or drinking a fifth of booze (unless we drive afterward). It is not against the law to destroy ourselves. Although we seldom commit any unlawful, anti-social act, believe me, compulsive overeating is an act of insanity.

My failure at controlling my life was what directed me to the First Step of this Program. The more I had tried to control, the less I could control. The more I tried to diet, the less I was able to diet. When I decided to give myself to this Program, *I gave my will over to God.* Then God gave me the will and the power *back* that enabled me to live. I now live with God's power, and He has given me control over food. That can happen on a daily basis through the Eleventh Step.

I decided at one point that I did not want to be unhappy anymore and that I would go to any lengths to be sane. To me, the difference between compulsive behavior and sanity lies in the choice that is made between one second and the next. Sanity means that just before you get into your compulsiveness, you recognize that you have time to make the decision *not* to be compulsive. During that split second before you act compulsively, you can see the situation and the consequences and choose not to carry out your compulsion. The difference between my former self and my present self is that I used to be into my compulsion before I really took a look at it. Now I can see it *before* I get into it, and in that second I have a choice. God's will shows us the choices we have. We can't ask for anything more.

We begin to sort out ways that work in our lives from ways that don't work. If we do one thing, we will feel good immediately, but terrible in the long run. If we do something else, we may not feel so good right away, but we will feel terrific in the long run. The first way — doing something that makes us feel good immediately — leaves us eventually feeling bad and guilty and anxious so that we eat and eat and eat over it. The second way — putting off immediate happiness in exchange for long-term happiness — may work better for us. Neither of these approaches is wrong or right; but we have the choice about how we want to feel.

We can choose to overeat or not to overeat. Overeating gives me immediate gratification, but I feel bad the rest of my life. Eating appropriately may give me immediate discomfort, but then I feel good the rest of my life.

More and more I choose ways that work in my life. More and more I choose to be sane.

We compulsive persons are fortunate in that we have been given physical signs, symbols that something major is wrong in our lives. We can even say that we are lucky to be alcoholics or to be fat. Those outward manifestations of inner wrongs are gifts from God. This Program invites people to be recovered, to say yes to life instead of continually plugging into their old miseries.

No one is under a curse — doomed to be fat. We do not have to let others determine how we feel. We do not have to be bitter and unfeeling, to hide our fears, or appear to be what we are not. If we can accept our real selves, we will have no need to be phony.

This Program guarantees my sanity if I commit myself to it. Because we were created to be happy, when we choose to be unhappy we are going against nature by manufacturing problems for ourselves. The symptom of our unhappiness is the fat we see on the outside. We are distorting the life God gave us because we are distorting the bodies He gave us.

In order to lose the necessary weight and keep it off, you must consider two essentials: abstinence and a Higher Power. To maintain your weight losses, you need to keep in "fit spiritual condition," as the Big Book calls it, by keeping a constant conscious contact with your Higher Power and by *being there* for others (the Twelfth Step). Spirituality is a concern for others, a reaching out to say, "What can I do for you today?" That is what keeping in fit spiritual condition means. If you really discover this spirituality for yourself, you *cannot* be fat.

You may know intellectually how to abstain, how to find a Higher Power, how to keep in fit spiritual condition, but whether you do or do not carry out these principles is up to you.

What led me to the Big Book was the fact that I couldn't keep my weight off, and others like me couldn't maintain their weight losses either.

If I am thin, but still as crazy in my food compulsion as I ever was, what has this Program proved? After studying the Big Book, I sat down and said, "God, do with me as you will. If you are going to make me fat again, I don't care. But fat or thin, I don't want food as a problem any more. I don't want to have to think about it or worry about it or have *anything* to do with it. I cannot handle food as a problem."

As soon as I said those words, I realized that, for the first time, I was taking the First Step. I was powerless over food. Food was no longer my god. The battle was over and my sanity was restored. Now the Program asks that I go and share the *recovery* and the *sanity* of this way of life.

If we have absolute trust in this Program and the willingness to be sane, if we humbly offer ourselves to our God, the promises of this Program are: we will know a new happiness; we will know peace and serenity; feelings of self-pity will disappear; fears of people and other insecurities will leave us; we will cease fighting automatically; we will be safe and protected; our compulsion will be removed.

There are two things we must add in our lives: pleasure and service. If we do not put these first, we will go back to eating and being fat.

But remember that the Program is not really about losing weight, but about becoming sane.

When you make the decision to live and to work the Twelve Steps of this Program, all of its promises can come true. Choose to recover through God as you understand Him.

Thin is not necessarily well. But if you are well, you will be thin.

Other Good Books for Weight-losers

If you found *Compulsive Overeater* helpful, you will want to know about these books, too.

From Alcoholics Anonymous World Services

Alcoholics Anonymous (the Big Book). This is the basic text of AA, in which members share their experiences of recovery. The strength and inspiration of its message, intended to help alcoholics, has been adapted by many others dealing with different compulsions, including food compulsion.

Twelve Steps and Twelve Traditions. Affectionately called "Twelve by Twelve" by members in AA and in other Twelve-Step groups, this is AA founder Bill W.'s classic explanation of the fellowship's principles of recovery and the traditions upon which the society is based.

From CompCare Publishers

Break Out of Your Fat Cell The Holistic Mind/Body Guide to Permanent Weight Loss by Jeane Eddy Westin, author of the best-selling *The Thin Book.* This looks at the problem of overweight from a

---

*These books may be purchased from Alcoholics Anonymous World Services, Inc., Box 459, Grand Central Station, New York, New York 10017. They also may be ordered from CompCare Publishers, 2415 Annapolis Lane, Suite 140, Minneapolis, Minnesota 55441, which stocks these AA classics as a service to customers. This does not in any way indicate an endorsement by AA of CompCare Publishers or of materials published or distributed by CompCare.

"whole person" point of view, relating successful weight loss to a positive self-image and offering practical strategies for survival in a thin chauvinist society. It helps weight-losers live complete satisfying lives *while* they take off the pounds.

Consider the Alternative by Lee M. Silverstein. The author-therapist, known nationally for his inspiring lectures and workshops, shares his personal story of recovery and synthesizes popular helping theories into a practical guide for living. This beautiful blend of humanity and therapy has been greeted with enthusiasm by experts like Albert Ellis, Joel Fort, William Glasser, John Powell, and Sidney B. Simon, who wrote the foreword.

A Day at a Time. CompCare's pocket-sized, contemporary book of daily readings, now with nearly a quarter of a million copies in print, includes thoughts and prayers for coping serenely with life's complexities. Its wisdom is helpful for anyone, but especially for those working Twelve-Step programs.

Laugh It Off by Jane Thomas Noland. Excerpted by *Cosmopolitan* magazine, this is used widely as a witty workbook by individual weight-losers and weight-loss groups. Funny essays, cartoons, slogans, jingles and puns underline a valuable message — that shedding pounds is a positive experience. This pep-talks wishful shrinkers into losing the equivalent of half a twin-bed mattress or a truck tire. It offers *actual* ways (along with a *trick* way — flip-page animation) to make the scale go down!

The Thin Book 365 Daily Aids for Fat-free, Guilt-free, Binge-free Living by Jeane Eddy Westin. Grateful weight-losers the world over have taken this book to heart and found daily inspiration in it, no matter what kind of weight-loss program they may be following. This much-loved book, now with over 85,000 in print, strikes at the core of the overweight's problem — sagging motivation — and keeps its readers on a thinning course. Excerpts have appeared in *Cosmopolitan* magazine in English- and foreign-language editions.

This Will Drive You Sane by Bill L. Little. Foreword by Albert Ellis. A warm-hearted therapist with a towering sense of humor, known for his on-the-air counseling sessions over CBS Radio KMOX out of St. Louis, backhandedly shows how to *get rid of* problems by explaining, in droll detail, how to *produce* them. Misery is not simply a state of being, but an art to be developed — and wallowed in! This humorous approach to everyday problems can ease the stress that often leads to overweight.

The Twelve Steps for Everyone . . . who really wants them. Originally written to interpret AA's Program for members of Emotional Health Anonymous (EHA), this sensitive book can help anyone find strength and healing through the Twelve Steps. Individuals and groups all over the country have found this interpretation of the Twelve Steps — now with over 100,000 in print — easy to understand and apply.

Ask us to send you a free CompCare Publishers catalog of books and other materials emphasizing a positive approach to life's problems, large and small. You'll find wise books, practical books, funny and inspirational books, on a broad range of topics. If you have questions, call us toll free at 800/328-3330. (Minnesota residents call 612/559-4800.)

CompCare®
publishers